THE OPENING UP
OF AMERICAN
EDUCATION
A SAMPLER

Ruskin Teeter

UNIVERSITY
PRESS OF
AMERICA

LANHAM • NEW YORK • LONDON

Copyright © 1983 by

University Press of America,™ Inc.

4720 Boston Way
Lanham, MD 20706

3 Henrietta Street
London WC2E 8LU England

ISBN (Perfect): 0-8191-3137-7
ISBN (Cloth): 0-8191-3136-9
LCN: 83-3647

TO MY PARENTS,

   Charles and Neva Taylor Teeter

Acknowledgements

During the years of working on this book, I acquired more than a few debts to friends and scholars, and it is now time to thank those who have so generously helped me. Professors Robert Reeser and Walter Brown of the University of Arkansas helped to create in me, many years ago, a love for education and history, and a sense that the lessons of history need not be dull or pedantic. They have been constantly at the back of my mind as I have offered my own views as to the way American public education has developed over the last 350 years. Dr. William Van Til, Coffman Distinguished Professor Emeritus of Education at Indiana State University has read parts of the manuscript and has made many helpful suggestions, as has Dr. William Preston Vaughn, Professor of History at North Texas State University. I have also to thank professors Dennis Engles, Jim Miller, Jean Greenlaw, Ruth Kurth and Barry Lumsden for reading and criticizing my work. Dr. Walter Sandefur, my department chair, has extended me every courtesy, to the point of scheduling my classes around a wholly unorthodox set of work habits. Miss Ellie Whitmore at my Inter-Library Loan desk has always found the books I have needed, and has thereby saved me much in the way of time and travel expense. Dr. Elmo Richardson, conservationist, biographer, and teacher *par excellence*, has been my editor, organizer, consultant and constant friend, and has guided me smoothly through the later stages of this work. Whatever merit is found in these pages owes mainly to those acknowledged above. The mistakes are wholly my own.

Acknowledgements

CONTENTS

Preface

It is almost a cliche to say that a nation's educational system reflects its fundamental beliefs in human values. Historians have certainly established that relationship. This volume is intended to illustrate the forms and functions of public schools throughout three and a half centuries of development. But the idea has not been to merely recapitulate a history. In order to bring far greater impact on the reader—whether student, teacher or parent—I have carefully chosen a score or more points in time when the *purpose* of education was shaken and redirected, sometimes by great social developments, but more often by the faith and persistance of an amazingly small number of crusaders.

Americans of today tend to view their past as a simpler, more flexible time, when solutions to social and economic problems were obvious, and therefore easier to accomplish. But the force of Puritanism, with its elitist convictions about the potential for human growth, dominated American thinking for nearly two centuries. It prevailed because it provided certainties and stabilities to a willingly uprooted people. Yet the daily existence of these growing populations was a quest for opportunities. Thus, it was "King Numbers" who continually encouraged—indeed demanded—reassessment and reform of all institutions. The heroes of these chapters are not the impersonal forces of quantities. They are men and women obsessed with the *qualities* of teaching. Better than legislators or merchants, they recognize the basic needs of the populations who inherit the promise of American life in each succeeding generation.

It is easier for us to acknowledge the wisdom of those reformers in the past than to admit to the soundness of arguments from their idealistic heirs in our own time. By following earlier problems and solutions up to the school crises of today, this book is intended to remind us of continuities, not only in substance but in procedure as well. The most important of these are the refurbishing of teacher training, the "education" of public officials, the expansion of curricula, and—more obvious than any—the adoption of new tools of learning. Students, parents and teachers of today should know full well, however, that even a whole phalanx of programs does not automatically prevail over the social bigotries that persist from the past. The closing chapters of this book provide an uncomfortable reminder of how the democratic purposes of American education must be sustained not only by court decisions and legislative mandates, but by wholesale public understanding that a continued "opening up" of the American school is the only direction possible in a democracy.

Ruskin Teeter

Denton, Texas
February, 1983

Introduction

Thousands of parents, teachers, and educational administrators are currently looking to the past to try to rediscover the fundamentals of education that seem to have been lost in our own time. In our future—shocked late 20th Century, the schools of an earlier America look to them like *terra firma*, like a solid earth of certainties amid the morass and erosion that now threaten learning. As part of an apparent new conservatism, there are increasing calls for returning to the basics: the 3 Rs, to rules, respect—even the hickory stick. Restore community control of schools, these advocates argue, by which they mean strengthen local determination of who shall attend which schools, what kind of teaching methods shall be used, and even what content shall be included in instruction.

In some quarters, this "back to" movement is labeled as reactionary, as basically ignorant and destructive in its motivation. Americans who hold separation of church and state to be one of the cornerstones of democracy discern more than just an aura of religious revivalism in these recent developments. There has been a marked increase in the number of private fundamentalist schools meaning to recreate the educational standards of the past. The supporters of these institutions demand tax credits or exemptions from legislatures and courts, arguing that they are religious in nature and purpose. Their critics, however, point to the obvious political implications involved in their teaching "morality" and "patriotism." Far more ominous than the contentions of both sides are the implications for the future of American education. The "back to" movement may be seen as an expression of citizen loss of confidence in public education. It may be worse than that: a rejection of the modern view of the essential goodness and potential talent of the child—and therefore of every citizen as well. Observers of the resurgent fundamentalism especially wonder how its advocates can encompass both Puritanism and a militant adherence to free economic enterprise in the same philosophy. Moreover, if their assumption of the child's (and man's) innate depravity recaptures the educational segment of American society, will it not also penetrate the political system as well?

Americans who are asking such questions may well find useful the truism that there is no better clue to the future than a study of the past. Like every institution of any society, the school fulfills and reflects the needs and purposes of populations. Our education has always been an expression of the great middle class and the work ethic of 17th and 18th Century origins. Indeed the "humanism" railed against by those who seem to know so little of their own history, was in fact an extension of those same values. An examination of the 350-year span of schooling in America documents an "opening up" process repeated in every generation. The limitations of the rural and small town school gave way to the larger dimensions of increasingly urbanized schools. Similarly, the academy with its "talented tenth" of white male society, was overwhelmed by schools for children of both sexes and many ethnic backgrounds—children of the "common man." The recent efforts to give Blacks and New Americans access to quality education is, in historical perspective, merely a continuation of that "opening up." These developments were, of course, brought about by the same kinds of struggles, by selfishness and courage, by solitary heroes and by "King Numbers," as is every other movement in human history. But they are less known because they were waged in smaller arenas, with fewer spectators and less coverage by the media. Because of the significance of their impact on the development of American democracy, they warrant re-examination, not as curiosa, but as evidence of the ways in which democratic education is always a foundation stone in the structure of the democratic society.

This volume intends to present a readable, relatively concise history of American education (precollege) from colonial times to the present. Its main theme suggests progress through the 350 years of school history in America in the gradual opening up of free public education to an increasingly large constituency, from the initial well-to-do and limited special student population, to the rural and poor and, later, blacks, females, etc. The history is designed to show the complex constellation of forces and obstacles along the way that shaped this expansion of free, publicly supported education. But more importantly, the volume can also serve as a basis for understanding the struggles that are currently going on in American education and to realize their historical roots. Its basic aim is to reach a broad audience of teachers and the public-at-large, in understanding the contributions of public education to our democracy.

ONE
The Marm's School

"Your child is never too young to go to hell."

A Looking Glass for Children
James Janeway, 1771

Puritan minister James Janeway's pointed reminder to parents epitomizes the climate of thought from which American education emerged. During most of the Colonial and early National periods, the school and the student were stepchildren in the structure of social life. A school was rarely a building constructed for the sole purpose of education, and it was usually furnished with minimal facilities for human occupancy, let alone learning. Largely ignorant teachers, themselves barely beyond childhood, regarded youthful spirit as evidence of the Devil and treated their charges with callousness at best, often subjecting them to arbitrary and sanctimonious brutality. In the language of the time, schools were "kept;" the word was an accurate description of the teaching method used. Information was "poured in" to the students as if they were only receptacles, then extracted by inquisition. Repetition and recitation permitted little in the way of inquiry or understanding. Even contemporary observers concluded that the system was largely a waste of time and that the only fortunate thing about it was the fact that it was seldom accessible to the great majority of children who lived outside of towns. Moreover, the records of the time indicate that such education was seldom compulsory or even "free."[1]

The first schools were part of the cycle of sun and weather that governed the lives of those who settled the iso-

1

lated rural areas of America. These one-room structures, usually painted white and resembling that other essential institution of society, the church, were populated by students only during the winter months. Schooling was a matter taken up only after the much more basic needs for sustaining life had been met. With the many chores children had to perform during the growing season, there simply wasn't enough time left over to give to books. But with the approach of the fall season and the autumnal equinox (around September 23), and with the gathering of crops and storing away of wintry hoards, the pace of farm life began to slacken. Now came the "off-season," along with increased social activities, fall festivals, shorter work days, and family holidays. And now, education, having taken its turn behind the very real business of living, could be dealt with and finally put to rights.

In the beginning, and particularly outside the towns, the few parents who were themselves literate enough to do so simply passed on whatever reading and writing skills they had to their children in whatever ways they knew. It can be imagined that their lessons were easily and quite naturally worked into the day-to-day routine of the winter season. On a rainy day, for example, mother would take down some printed alphabet letters pasted on a piece of board from her living room wall and gather the smallest of her brood about her near the fire. Then, perhaps calling upon her own childhood, she invented games to the delight of her children, and thus sweetened the ugly pill of learning. Pointing to letters of the alphabet, coaxing, wheedling, romping and laughing, she would "wring out" from them the answers to her questions. Her rewards for learning were praise, kisses, and caresses, but also hot gingerbread, fruit pies and tarts, perhaps intuitively making for her children the connection between learning, or work, and life.

After supper and evening chores, an educated father might gather his children about the fireplace for family hour, Bible reading, conversation and worship. And to impart his love for learning and religion, he might help an older child read aloud from the family Bible the stories of David and Goliath, Samson and Delilah, Noah and the flood,

2

Daniel and the lion's den and Jonah and the fish. Or wishing to dwell on the subject of human frailties, morals and virtues, he might help with the reading of the stories from Aesop of the tortoise and the hare, the lion and the mouse, the lazy grasshopper, the fox and the grapes, and the goose that laid the golden egg.

But literacy was at a premium in early America, and few indeed were the number of parents who could do much more than read a business sign or advertisement, or put to paper their own names, or fashion a crudely written message. Most parents, in fact, were but a generation or two removed from the dark, dirty and violent cities of 17th Century Europe. They or their fathers or grandfathers, had lived a good part of their lives in tightly-knit, socially combustible neighborhoods, clumped together along narrow, smelly, cobbled streets, which were breeding grounds for disease. They had lived desperately, often in irreducible and irreversible circumstances. Superstition, not learning, had been their world. They had wallowed in ignorance, mystification and bewilderment at the natural world. Theirs had been a world of bewitchment, charms, chants, magic stones, and mumbo-jumbo gibberish. It had taken almost all of their conniving just to keep the Devil and his fallen angels at bay. They had had little use for learning, and little in the way of background or tradition for learning.[2]

Primarily for these reasons, schooling developed slowly in early America. Education surely was not uppermost in the minds of the earliest settlers. There was no school at Plymouth for more than 50 years, even though 32 children had been aboard the Mayflower; and there was no school at Jamestown, the first permanent settlement in America, for almost a hundred years. With today's emphasis on education, it is difficult to imagine just how minor and subordinate a role school actually played in the everyday lives of most of the early Americans. There were towns and ships to build, and families to feed and clothe. There seemed almost no practical use for the study of grammar, language and the classics. In fact, education *per se* was mistrusted by many of the boys growing up in the heady atmosphere of raw frontier towns. There were gambling dens, ale houses and brothels in

Boston—as well as the first grammar (secondary) school in America—long before there was a system of permanent schoolhouses. Something about education seemed to these tusslers as unmanly, prideful, affected and snobbish. With construction and growth all about, the study of "dead" languages seemed especially a lost labor. For the most part, colonial youth were "innocent of books," as the saying went (in the long-ago innocence of America itself) before the harsher word "illiterate" came into vogue.

Even after the passage of laws mandating schools, such as the Massachusetts laws of 1642 and 1647, schools had very slow growth.[3] By 1640, there were still only seven schools among the 20,000 education-loving English Puritans who had migrated to New England. Sixty years later, after 93 years of settlement on the continent, there were still fewer than 30 grammar schools in the whole of America. Only about 20% of the towns mandated by law to keep schools actually did so.

Schoolkeeping began in early America in the way of the early "marm" or women's schools. Boys *and* girls went to these schools, usually at age 6 or 7, usually for one or two years at two or three months per year, and usually from 9 in the morning until 3 in the afternoon, six days per week. These marm schools actually provided more in the way of motherly care and keeping than in the study of the rudiments of language and arithmetic. Very little time at all was given to any formal instruction, since the women were busy throughout the day with their homemaking chores—making soap and candles, cleaning, cooking, etc. Students even helped in these chores; boys were often put to shelling peas or beans, and girls to sewing or preparing and serving snacks and hot lunches. Marms mingled their teacher-nurse-mother duties, ingeniously keeping good order while mixing a little learning inside the house with a lot of play outside (community standards permitting) in large fenced yards. They did not often rely on the hickory stick for discipline, as did men teachers of the higher levels, but upon their natural or maternal understanding of children. There were a few occasions when severe punishment might be meted out, but usually the marm's steel sewing thimble mounted atop a

4

strong middle finger, and used for thumping heads, was quite sufficient to quell the animal vigors and nervous temperaments of rowdy boys.

In the earliest years of settlement, very few children attended any one marm school at a given time. Few homes were larger than 14-by-16 feet in size, and then they were filled with the marm's family, and with space-consuming looms, flax wheels, cradles, churns, stools and other furniture. Probably five or six children per marm was a maximum school size during most of the 17th Century. As homes became larger and as other non-residential facilities became available, class sizes increased to upwards of 15 or 20 students per school. But most children attended no school at all, for the teaching of simple rudiments was considered a family, not a public, matter.

Students arrived at the marm school shortly after morning milking and feeding chores had been done. After a devotional, they were put to their studies—memorizing the alphabet and drawing letters in sand (there was very little paper available in the colonies during the 17th Century). They pronounced words, ciphered, read and spelled. Often marms made games of words; to spell the word "Massachusetts," for example, children would chant a ditty, "MA crooked letter, crooked letter A. . . " The best learning undoubtedly took place on cold rainy days when marms and children could not work outside, and when they were caught up with indoor work. On such days, children worked contentedly before a cheerful fire laid in a deep cave-like fireplace complete with heavy stone chimney. As they worked along, each at a different task and pace, the marm might brew a pot of spiced tea as a treat. Later she would warm the lunches the children had brought, or serve one of her own making—perhaps roasted sweet potatoes topped with melted butter and brown sugar. Then, after lunch, the children would play or rest, and then return for an early afternoon reading session. For snacks the marm might roast apples or nuts in the fireplace, or bake gingerbread as a reward for the children's good work and behavior. Then, sometime after mid-afternoon, the children would leave for the day in time to complete their wood and water carrying chores at home before dark.

Those marms who were married to ministers or to wealthy merchants possessed a better-than-average intellect and education, and by virtue of their access to books and men of learning, were able to bring something of an informal curriculum to their students. At least they could reinforce much of the learning and erudition of the day. Learned men, for example, knew that the study of astronomy, which was then a mixture of medieval astrology and the writings of Claudius Ptolemy, could go a long way toward helping people sidestep calamity, mishap and hard fate; and it is reasonable to expect that their wives passed on such attitudes to the children they taught. "Feiry-tayled" comets dried up the earth's moisture, some marms taught, and gave notice of impending droughts, hot winds, crop failures and fevers. It followed that if the stars foretold natural events, they also foretold the individual fates of men; and it was then but a step away to say that if God had left messages in the sky, he had left them on earth as well, and that it behooved men to be on the lookout for God's signatures, his clues, signals and broad hints as to how man's health and happiness could be maintained or improved.

The kidney bean's odd shape, for example, was a hint, a signal from God that it was intended as a curative for problems with that organ of the body. Snakefat was likewise an antidote for poison, and powdered frog skins were obviously a remedy for skin eruptions, poxes, blemishes, etc. Marms who were married to physicians may have passed on some of the popular physiology of the day. Any illness was simply a disturbance of the four body humors, and to readjust them was but a matter of letting blood, taking care to draw equal amounts from both sides of the body to prevent an imbalance. There were other aspects of the marm's informal curriculum as well. They warned and frightened their children of the bogeyman—or in the words of Samuel Sewall, presiding judge at the Salem witchcraft trials, "stirred children up dreadfully to seek God." Children were taught that they were not just born in sin, they were conceived in sin. In the eyes of God, a leading minister of the day told them, they were as "despicable as vipers, likewise

6

beautiful when small." One of the community's primary expectations of the marms was that they help bring children to God at the earliest possible moment so that if they died young they might still go to heaven. The modern-day "now I lay me down to sleep" prayer harks back to that time when the doctrine of infant damnation was widely accepted. Marms no doubt taught this prayer to the few children who failed to learn it at home. Most marms were gentle and reassuring with children on the subject of the possibility that they might spend an eternity in hell, and they echoed their preachers' sentiments that condemned children, by virtue of their youth, would still probably get the "easiest room in hell." But a few shrieked on the subject, and they benumbed and petrified children beyond description. Many parents, impressed by such behavior, sought out marms who were especially good at instilling this fear in children.

Few marms possessed much in the way of learning or erudition. Most were of the yeoman class, and few were refined in either thought or manner. To indicate their lowly caste, they were addressed as "goodwife" or "goody" so and so. Many dipped snuff and swore, and not a few nipped along throughout the day on New England or Santa Cruz rum. Favorite obscenities were "by my soul," and "as I am a Christian," and few were the children who could resist rushing home to tell of their indiscretions, much to the outrage of the parents.

The best known fixtures of marm schools were "absey" books. These were really not books at all, but single sheets of expensive paper on which were printed the alphabet in large and small letters, the Lord's Prayer, and the 10 digits. Sometimes the Roman numerals, simple syllables and the vowels were also given. This was the device which marms used to teach reading before paper and books were plentiful in the colonies. This sheet was mounted on a thin piece of paddle-shaped wood, about five inches long and two inches wide. To protect the paper, a frosty transparent protective covering was applied. Since it was made of animal hooves, fish scales, or snake or lizard skins, a substance called "horn," the books were called "hornbooks." But Shakespeare, and most marms and children in England, where the books originated, called them "absey" books. The usual procedure was for the marm to take the "book" from the child's neck or waist, where it was appended for easy carrying, and to point out a letter or number to the child. The child then identified the character, and in doing so was sometimes rewarded with gingerbread cookies baked in the shape of the letters or numbers identified.[4]

As paper and printing became more available in early America, marms replaced hornbooks with the New England Primer. It was the most widely used textbook in the country throughout the 18th Century, and it was popular in schools even into the 19th Century. More than three million copies of the text were sold, but more than 20 million children learned to read from it, several sharing a single volume. The primer was five inches long, three inches wide, and contained about 80 pages. Because of its religious content, it was often called the "little Bible." It was not the book's purpose to celebrate life or amuse children. Rather, the theme of young death ran constantly throughout its rhymed alphabet pages: "While youth do cheer, death may be near;" "No youth we see, from death is free;" "As runs the hourglass, our life doth pass;" and "Xerxes did die, and so must I." Other verses instilling certain attitudes and values in children included: "The idle fool is whip'd at school;" "Job feels the rod, yet blesses God;" and "My book and heart shall never part." Words such as "abomination," "mortification," "purification," and "humiliation" reiterated these lessons. The primer also contained the Apostles' Creed, the Lord's Prayer, and a series of questions and answers about the Bible. As a means of catching the children's attention, each book was prefaced with an illustration of one "John Rogers" being burned at the stake, his wife and nine children looking sorrowfully on. According to the primer, the martyr Rogers was "burnt at Smithfield, February 14, 1554." But although millions of children believed the story, it was later determined to be a hoax. Today the New England Primer offends the sensibilities of many who do not understand the modern school's ecclesiastical heritage. Schools did not begin to drift from these religious moorings until after the American Revolution.[5]

During the 18th Century, marm schools slowly evolved into publicly supported reading and writing schools in towns, and into "district" schools in the rural areas. Now, women began to leave their homes, which could accomodate but a few children, and "keep" schools of primary grade in buildings set up especially for purposes of education. They never aimed beyond mere literacy and simple arithmetic, however. They did do much to socialize children and teach them good manners, and they served as feeder schools to the Latin preparatory or grammar or secondary schools. Children who showed a proficiency for language or who could memorize well were channeled by these marms into secondary schools. But for 8 out of 10 children, completion of marm school at age 7 or 8 meant the completion of their formal education. The most successful of them could read and write and do simple sums.

It is easy to underestimate the significance of the old marm schools. Here was about the only place the child of average means could study his own language—the roots, syllables, vowel sounds and word structure of the English language—as opposed to those of classical languages. It is also easy to overlook these marms' contributions to American culture. With only a smattering of knowledge themselves, and with a lack of facilities, books, paper, and pencils, and for the most miserly of wages, they brought together a few children from their neighborhoods and communities and taught them some simple ways of using words and numbers. What is more, they relied not on training but on their feminine aptitude for working with children. Their schools were generally happy places; the next best thing, the children said, to "going to grandma's house."

There were other kinds of schools in colonial America where children learned to read and write. Private schools were much in evidence throughout the period, and in general they were superior to the schools just discussed. There were dancing and fencing academies and boarding and business schools for boys and girls. There were morning, day and evening, Latin, French and English schools, many approved and licensed by town authorities. Some were pretentious and superficial, advertising as many as 13

9

subjects taught by a single master at "easie rates and as speedy as may be." Private schools also offered entry into the Latin schools and sometimes supplanted them. Among their more popular offerings were grammar, reading, accounting, algebra, geography, banking, shorthand, polite languages, government, diction, music, cookery, waxwork, Japanning, quillwork, needlework, glass painting, drawing, tapestry, horsemanship and dance. Sometimes such schools were bought by towns and converted to publicly supported town schools.[6]

Long after the Revolution, millions of school children would continue to use the hard benches and primers that had characterized the marm's school of the Colonial period. But many would also have a second experience in education, the grammar school. That institution offered a far more worldly curriculum and required the services of someone who was more educated and less encumbered than the simple, gentle marm.

Sources
One

[1] The ambivalence of early settlers toward education is in Samuel Chester Parker, *The History of Modern Elementary Education* (n.p. 1912; reprint ed., Totowa, N.J.: Littlefield, Adams & Co., 1970), pp. 55 ff. The rate of growth of early colonial schools is in William Herbert Small, *Early New England Schools* (Boston: Ginn & Company, 1914), p. 30.

[2] Descriptions of social, cultural, intellectual and economic life in England immediately prior to emigration to North America, and the conditions of knowledge and education, particularly the mystification and bewilderment of the masses at natural phenomena are in *Shakespeare's England* (Oxford University Press, 1916), pp. 224-250; 413-443. The transit of knowledge from England to America is in Edward Eggleston, *The Transit of Civilization from England to America in the 17th Century* (New York: D. Appleton & Co., 1901), pp. 5-65. For accounts of the *real* early Boston - viz. more of the same sin and corruption John Winthrop had despaired of in England, see Darrett B.

Rutman, *Winthrop's Boston: Portrait of a Puritan Town, 1630-1649* (Chapel Hill: University of North Carolina Press, 1965), pp. 3-8; 12 ff. Rutman sets the scene for America's first school, juxtaposing it against a seaport town given to outbreaks of the French Disease, not against a gloom and doom city of God. See also Alfred Bushnell Hart (ed.), *The American Nation: A History* (New York: Harper & Brothers, 1904) v. 1, pp. 216-73. The subtitle is from James Janeway's *Looking Glass for Children* which he described as "an exact account of the conversion . . . holy lives and joyous deaths of several young children . . . in whom the fear of God was remarkably budding before they died."

³ The Ezekial Cheever school of early Boston is in Phillips Brooks, *The Oldest School in America* (Boston: Houghton, Mifflin & Co., 1885), pp. 3-13. Brooks is a descendant of the Phillips family that founded Andover and Exeter academies, two foremost American secondary schools.

⁴ The hornbook was used in England as early as 1442. It was standard equipment in English schools by the 1500's. It was used only in England and America, although a similar teaching tool, the alphabet board, was found throughout Europe. These were not covered with horn. Fewer than 200 hornbooks are known to exist anywhere in the world. Most are in private collections. Crudely etched on the back of a hornbook in the British Museum are the words, "what more could be wished than to be able to read and spell." Alphabet molds in which gingerbread letters were baked still turn up occasionally at rural English bake shops. They, too are collector's items. The educational and social position of colonial marms is in Alice M. Earle, *Child Life in Colonial Days* (New York: The Macmillan Co., 1932) pp. 90-95. See also Anne Hollingsworth Wharton, *Colonial Days and Dames* (Philadelphia: J. B. Lippincott, 1895) pp. 11-98; 125-52. For descriptions of colonial libraries and books see Lewis B. Wright, *The Cultural Life of the American Colonies: 1607-1763* (New York: Harper and Row, 1962) pp. 98-153. See also Andrew W. Tuer, *Pages and Pictures from Forgotten Children's Books* (London: The Leadenhall Press, 1898; reprint ed., Detroit: Singing Tree Press, 1969) pp. 337-

402. For general works on colonial education, see Sheldon S. Cohen, *A History of Colonial Education 1607-1776* (New York: John Wiley and Sons, 1974). For the "old deluder Satan" act and other such laws, see Nathaniel B. Shurtleff (ed.) *Records of the Governor and Company of the Massachusetts Bay in New England* (Boston; n.p., 1853) v. II, pp. 6-7. Andrew Tuer's *History of the Hornbook* (New York: Benjamin Bloom, 1968) gives accounts of the hornbook and the New England Primer.

[5] The best work on the New England Primer is Paul Leicester Ford's *The New England Primer: A History of its Origin and Development* (New York: Teachers College, Columbia University, 1962). For the Puritan view of the child, see Sanford Fleming, *Children and Puritanism* (New Haven: Yale University Press, 1933).

[6] Descriptions of non-public schools in early America, both elementary and secondary, are in R. F. Seybolt, *The Private Schools of Colonial Boston* (Cambridge: Harvard University Press, 1935; reprint ed., New York: Arno Press, 1969) pp. 83-92. See also Geroge E. Littlefield, *Early Schools and School Books of New England* (Boston: The Club of Odd Volumes, 1904).

TWO
The Grammar School Master

"He had . . . a happy mixture of pliability and perserverance in his nature . . . and he ever bore in mind the golden maxim, 'spare the rod and spoil the child.' Ichabod Crane's scholars certainly were not spoiled."

Legend of Sleepy Hollow
Washington Irving

The colonial schoolmaster was not the stereotype popularized by Irving's anti-hero. In reality, he usually took personal pride in and social status from his position. Whether he wore homespun or broadcloth, dressed in embroidered waistcoat or sported an ivory-headed cane, everyone in the community knew him. Whether or not he inspired the elders, he represented a degree of accomplishment to their children. Schoolmasters were therefore understandably sensitive about their reputations and appearances. Whatever class or station they came from, they tried to emulate the best men of the past and present. Some shared in businesses or marriages that enabled them to fulfill their larger view of themselves. Thereby they also became landowners and pillars of the community. Many owned cows, oxen and rental property, and were given honored pews in their churches. That was true of those who had come to America by way of the great English-language universities at Cambridge, Aberdeen, Oxford and Glasgow. But even those who had been sold off ship's deck as servants to pay their passage often had some familiarity with literature and language, ancient and modern. About the only thing grammar school masters shared in common was their

13

gender; all were men. To be sure, a few resembled the teacher of American lore. They were so dignified as to be stern and humorless. They dressed in black and taught and prayed in solemn tones. They could summon the Lord and stare down the Devil. And they could pray away the sins of youth with conviction and persuasion. But most school masters were simple, earthy, country people, members of the working class who owned small plots of land and draft animals and produced their own food and clothing. Not a few were lame or otherwise disabled, shut out from more physical work. And almost all doubled as carpenters, cobblers, inn-keepers and handymen, since teaching was almost never considered a full-time occupation. There was also a large class of itinerant or vagabond teachers who roamed throughout the South during the winter months. Many of these could barely read and write and were much given to gambling, drinking and debauchery.

The colonial teacher was usually young, sometimes still a lad of 17 or 18, just graduated from one of the universities and waiting perhaps for a suitable church post to open up. Just as often, he was only 14 or 15 years of age and had only a grammar school education. Not a few were so young that they themselves played with the other children at recess. Many lived in poor, sometimes squalid circumstances—in church steeples, or in a homeowner's shed, or in a small attic in the school building itself. Pay was meager, and depended not so much on the teacher's fitness and training as on the community's ability and willingess to pay. Even when willing to pay, communities often had to renege on their original contracts because of financial exigencies. Sometimes they were two or three years in arrears in paying their teachers. While cash payments were small and sometimes few and far between, they were just as likely to be made in Portuguese, Dutch or Spanish coins—pieces of eight or Ryalls—as in Boston shillings. For these reasons, masters were often more than willing to take their pay in other emoluments. Students often paid their way with free labor, firewood, candles or animal skins. And "country pay"—mutton, wheat, sugar, malt, butter, apples, satin and nails—more often than not made up a good portion of the master's pay.

The Dutch school established at New Amsterdam (New York City) in the 1640's near what is now the intersection of Wall and Broad streets, and still in operation at a nearby location, allowed its masters to perform almost any kind of work that was not "reproachful" to help make ends meet. The Dutch masters there regularly cut hair, treated wounds, wrote obituaries and hoed gardens. They also did some church work—assisted at services, visited the sick, or rang the church bell—for pocket money. Sometimes a master's pay was in the form of the loan of a cow or a work animal, or he might be exempt from paying taxes, or given free rent, or permitted to feed his livestock from community stores, or permitted to use the school building for private tutoring. Masters acted as town clerks, boarded their students who lived far away, and even dug graves to supplement their meager teaching income. Sometimes towns simply gave masters *carte blanche* to collect whatever they could from students and a promise to make up the difference up to an agreed amount.

A vital factor in the pay system for colonial masters was the matter of respectability. Many were willing to give up prospects of better paying work and even to live in a state of genteel poverty in return for the appearance, if not the substance of respectability in the town or the church. The authorities of that first school in Manhattan, for example, ordered their townsmen to "acknowledge and respect" the Dutch masters in every way; to do nothing to "molest, disturb or ridicule" them, and to give them every assistance and deliver them "from every painful sensation." Acceptance of genteel poverty to gain respectability was, of course, the choice of those who valued orthodoxy and conformity, both political and religious. The "go-along and get-along" personalities of many school masters also signified their provincialism and, in some cases, their dim-wittedness.

A large part of the pay of masters who taught outside the towns was taken up in "free" room and board. The practice of "boarding around," or living in the homes of students as partial pay, began in colonial times and continued right up into the 1930's and 1940's. It was often a painful experience, especially if the master was in a home sending four or five students to school. Indeed, the length of time a master boarded with a family was tied to the number of that family's children whom he taught—the more children, the longer his stay with them. The frequent change in diet and lodging must have been uncomfortable, to say the least. The necessity of keeping up (or refraining from) a conversation—that is, the loss of privacy and independence—must have driven many from the profession.[1]

This excerpt from a diary of a Vermont school master documents the vagaries of such life in the students' homes of early America:

> *Monday.* Went to board at Mr. B's; had baked goose for dinner; suppose from its size, thickness of skin, it must have been one of the first settlers of Vermont. Supper—cold goose and potatoes. Family consisting of man, good wife, daughter, four boys, Pompey the dog, and a brace of cats.
> *Tuesday.* Cold gander for breakfast, swamp tea and nutcake—the latter some consolation. Dinner—the leg of the goose done up warm. Supper the other leg—cold.
> *Wednesday.* Cold goose for breakfast; complained of sickness and could eat nothing. Dinner—wings of goose warmed up. Dreaded supper all afternoon. Supper—hot Johnny cake; felt greatly revived. Very cold night. Couldn't keep warm. Got up and stopped the broken window with my coat.
> *Thursday.* Cold goose again. Much discouraged to see the goose not half gone. Went visiting for dinner and supper. Slept elsewhere for the night. Had pleasant dreams.
> *Friday.* Dinner—cold goose and potatoes, the latter very good.
> *Saturday.* Cold goose and hot Indian Johnny cake. Didn't keep school this afternoon. Weighed and found I had lost six pounds. Grew alarmed. Had a talk with Mr. B. and concluded I had boarded out his share.[2]

With all forms of pay and perquisites, the best paid schoolmasters of colonial times earned about the same income as skilled laborers. An exceptional case was Ezekiel Cheever, master at the Boston school for 38 years and perhaps the best known of all the colonial masters. Cheever left an estate with a current market value of about $200,000. But he taught until he was 94.

Perhaps the best characterization of the colonial teacher was the aforementioned Mr. Cheever. He had an excellent classical education and a top-rate mind. He published two books, one of which became the definitive American-published Latin textbook of the 17th Century. Still, he was a believer in witchcraft and never spoke out against the Salem witchhunters. Playwright Arthur Miller gave his name to a character in *The Crucible*.

Cheever was an excellent pedagogue—perhaps because he loved his boys completely. He not only worked with their minds, he wrestled with the Devil for their souls. But "Zeke," as they called him behind his back, had neither a sunny disposition nor an amiable spirit. Indeed, he did not suffer fools gladly. When he looked out at his boys he saw sinners of every stripe, and he flogged them mercilessly to drive the Devil away. Even into his eighties, Cheever would knock boys to the floor with his fist, then pounce upon them and pray fervently for their souls. Into his nineties, he was still strong enough to whip one boy (at random) per day, and then depend on him to settle accounts with all who had misbehaved, and who he would have whipped if he had had the strength. Up until the day he died at age 94, still firmly measuring out the Latin conjugations *do, dare, dedi, datum,* he was a terror; the better part of the love the boys had for him, as many later acknowledged, was simple fear. During his catnaps after lunch, only the most foolhardy ventured the slightest mischief. He was the gray eminence of Boston, the indisputable authority on all things academic.

Community requirements concerning teachers' moral character were not merely Puritanical, they were often wise as well. A number of teachers of the colonial period were unquestionably gamblers, fighters and drunken, profane womanizers. Very few of this class could manage their finances; many were indentured servants on the run from their employers, and newspapers of the period often carried advertisements warning readers to be on the lookout for this or that "runaway schoolmaster." Young adventurers, rascals and shattered souls just passing through kept schools all over colonial America. In the course of a year, one such teacher might offer his services to several communities.

Perforce, the best of the Colonial teachers would not be considered very effective by today's standards. They spent most of their time listening to recitations, and duly ordering: "translate the next 15 lines," or "solve the next 25 problems." Multiplication tables were memorized forward, backward, and "skip-wise." When not chanting *do, dare, dedi, datum*, they were studying the 208 principal bones of the human body, generalizing on the 5 races of mankind, naming the English kings in order, or describing the nine Muses. More "practical" assignments required students to "bound Norway" (name the countries bordering it), or tell how many square miles it contained. Practical, in fact, were questions familiarizing them with the seas, bays and gulfs on maps of the contained hemisphere, and computations of longitude, given an eight hour difference of time between London and some point in America. Many roots were squared and much interest was compounded. Another practical exercise required students to plot the best route by which tea might be shipped from the Bay of Bengal to Philadelphia.

As a result, schoolkeeping was humdrum, a matter of going around the same circles year after year, conducting drills in subjects, many of which little relation to the actual lives of their pupils. The system did not require masters to do much more than listen to recitation. As a result, they did their work mechanically, and many were boring, moralistic, platitudinous dolts. Teaching became a refuge for routine minds and as such wasted many of the talents of both masters and their pupils.

From most schoolmasters, the thing most conscientiously given the students was discipline. Although modern psychology would explain zealous discipline as sexually motivated, it was an essential concern of those generations. Children were believed to possess a certain "stubberness and stoutness" of mind which arose from "naturall pride."

18

Their pride, wrote clergyman John Robinson, had to be "broken and beaten down" so that the foundation of the child's education could be laid in "humilitie and tractableness." It was commendable that a horse be "stout and stomackfull," Robinson wrote, but who would "want his child like his horse in his brutishness?" Only when the spirit of the child (like the horse) had been broken, Robinson believed, could education truly begin.

The stern repressions employed by colonial schoolmasters were, of course, the continuation of centuries of tradition. Monks had appeared before their classes in the monastic schools of medieval Europe with rods and sticks, and their custom of administering drubbings was transplanted to the early grammar schools of Elizabethan England. One early piece of evidence attesting to a popular demand for strict discipline in English schools is a letter, dated 1457, from Agnes Paston, commanding her 16 year old son's London schoolmaster to "trewly belassch" him if he misbehaved. She would rather see him "beryed than lost for defaute." She proudly related that she herself beat her marriageable daughter, sometimes twice a day, and had "broken her head" in two or three places. Even Lady Jane Grey, the "nine-day Queen" of England, was "sharply taunted," "cruelly threatened," and punished with "pinches, nips and bobs," as a child. Two centuries later, the tradition was still strong in English schools. Samuel Johnson told of severe floggings from his schoolmaster who was "very wrong-headedly severe," and who shouted as the boy was whipped: "This I do to save you from the gallows." Even in the late 19th Century, the young Winston Churchill was beaten so severely that he had to be withdrawn from Harrow.

This tradition of school discipline made its way to the American colonies with sharp refinements. Cats-of-nine tails, birch sticks, and flappers (leather straps attached to pliable handles) were used for whippings, and these were often applied about the head. Ears were boxed, children were made to kneel on dried peas, noses and tongues were pinched by split branches, and "whispering sticks," (wooden gags) were tied in mouths as punishment for talking. Sometimes the soles of the children's feet were beaten. In the context of these severities, a student made to wear a cap with bells on it was a happy one. Other embarrassments ranged from leg-irons and handcuffs to dunce caps and placards. Students could also be tied inside cotton sacks and hung to tree limbs. One of the first teachers at Harvard hired two ushers to hold his 14 year old victims fast while he meted out justice. If the boys broke loose, the ushers were then flogged.[3]

The practice of schooling was most advanced in New England and the Middle Colonies of New York and Pennsylvania. But with the exception of Maryland these schools were seldom tried and seldom lasted in the South. The decentralization of population and greater distances characteristic of that region partly accounted for that record. But it was also due to be a general distrust of free education held by colonial leaders in the early period. Governor William Berkeley of Virginia, for example, wrote the Lord Commissioners of Foreign Plantations in 1671 thanking God that "there are no free schools and printing" in America, and hoping that "we shall not have these for a hundred years." Learning and printing had only brought "disobedience and heresy" into the world, he wrote. "God keep us from both." A more famous statement of sentiment was the reply of the Lord Commissioners to a Virginia preacher who asked for a school for the souls of the children: "Damn your souls, grow tobacco!"

Yet there is solid evidence that a lively interest in higher education existed in the South from the very beginning. The first "university" in the country (the title was pretentious) was established at Henricopolis, Virginia, years before Harvard was founded. A feeder school had been planned for it at a nearby settlement, hopefully named Charles City, to be called the East Indy school, and it was to be supported from the rental income on one thousand acres of land. A school master had already been engaged and had probably sailed for Virginia when an Indian uprising completely wiped out the entire settlement. After the carnage there, plans for a school were abandoned, and thereafter education developed very slowly in the South. But it was the lack of towns that most impeded the devlopment of education in the South. There were a few small settlements like Charles City

20

throughout that vast undeveloped frontier. But for a span of ninety years the only incorporated town in Virginia was Jamestown. What learning there was in the region was a catch-as-catch-can proposition. Groups of small planters would hire itinerant teachers for winter terms of one or two months. Church groups and planters' wives conducted a few schools; and college students exploring the frontier settlements of the South brought a measure of literacy and learning to those would-be communities. The vagabond teachers were often likeable minstrel types, and therefore attractive as teachers. They could sing and dance and tell stories; and they could read and write and cipher to the rule of three. A very few were excellent scholars.

With time, more permanent facilities such as the Symmes School and the Eaton School were established in the South, and Symmes at least, for most of its 100-year existence, was tuition free to needy and hardship cases. Symmes was established by terms of a will leaving milk cows and land to a community for the support of a school. Similar wills became commonplace in the South, and the income generated by bequests of slaves, farms and cattle supported many schools. These were called "cow and calf" schools. Many had long lives. Field schools were increasingly prevalent in the South. Kept by itinerant school masters for one- or two-month terms, they usually met in run-down cotton or tobacco sheds. George Washington attended two such schools for just under two months and then ended his school career at age 13. Grammar schools of the New England variety were almost never found in the South. Planters either hired tutors or sent their children abroad for their schooling, or simply ignored the idea altogether. Mary Ball, for example, later to become the mother of George Washington, was taught at home by a Cambridge graduate. But the great majority of children received no schooling whatever, nor did they want or miss school. Finally, by the end of the Colonial period, sons and daughters of the upper class were attending a few day schools and boarding schools on a very limited basis.

Schools in the Colonial settlements—North and South— were regarded as the stepchildren of the body politic. If laws mandated a school for every 100 families, as was often the case in New England, towns might choose to gerrymander their boundaries so as to include fewer than the 100 families. Or they might pay for a master but not a building. Indeed, the idea that schools were second only to churches in order of construction in the new colonies is erroneous: the meeting house, the grist mill, the armory, even the tavern, brothel, and gaminghouse were built first.

Where schools were constructed, however, they provided a welcome retreat from the world and sometimes even a few amenities. The schoolhouse was generally a small structure. It had an eight-foot ceiling, one or two fireplaces finished with brick and a stone chimney. It was here that students warmed lunches of mince pies and bean soup, or roasted slices of pork over the open fire. But even with two fireplaces, schools were usually cold in the winter, as blue noses and chattering jaws attested. Buildings were usually constructed first of pine logs, then later covered by brick. Windows were few, and seldom were they covered with glass. One ladder rose to an upper chamber where the master lived, and another led to the bell tower. Furnishings were rough-hewn and meager, and equipment such as spheres, cubes, pyramids, prisms, globes, blackboards and maps were virtually unknown. The Faber pencil, which came to be a standard feature in American schools, did not appear until the 1760's, and paper was so scarce and expensive that it was seldom used. The few who could afford it acquired almost microscopic writing for economy's sake. Even slates were scarce in the early grammar schools and ciphering was usually done on birch bark. Sand tables were also used for writing at many schools. Sand was spread thinly on a black surface, the edges of which were raised three or four inches. Leather smoothers were used to even out the sand each time the table was used. To these facilities came boys aged 8 to 15, starting out each winter morning at the "un-Christian hour of 6," as one of them later described it. Classes continued after lunch until 6 at night, and students were then dismissed with the command "Exeatis." There were no recesses or extra-curricular activities, but one afternoon each month might be given over to play and recreation, depending upon the master's mood, temperament and work ethic. Half-holidays were sometimes given to honor a visiting dignitary.

The first Latin school in America was established in Boston in 1635. It was a moving school: that is, it was kept in different parts of the town for a month or two at a time to keep down wrangling and bickering over who had the shortest walk to school. This moving school met in homes; the first school building in Boston was not erected until 20 years later.[4]

Despite its reputation as a fortress of solemnity and oppressive formalities, its harsh, sometimes brutal discipline, and its almost useless curriculum, the Latin grammar school reigned supreme for the first 150 years of American life. At the end it came to outshadow and outrival all other private, ecclesiastical and charitable educational schemes in the country combined. Thus, the old schools socialized, moralized and catechized. They preached, indoctrinated and converted. They disciplined and conditioned young boys, and in the end they pounded their charges into mental and spiritual shape by stuffing their heads with theology, facts, rules and knowledge.

Latin schools touched upon many subjects such as English composition and literature, mathematics, philosophy, Greek and science. But the main emphasis by far was given to the study of grammar—Latin grammar, that is, so that the literature of the Romans, which was thought to be the best in the world, could be read in the original. Language, the leaders of that age believed, was the most significant tool yet devised by man for his own uplift. It separated man from lower animals. With it he could develop and communicate ideas. Language gave him insight, and with insight, he could improve his lot. Since the Romans had built the greatest civilization the world had ever known, it only followed that their literature held the key to how civilizations were created. That literature would be read in the original, for translations, which were widely available, left room for error. They also sullied the beauty and style of the original. To be truly educated, to truly understand, only the original writing mattered. It was not just the literature that was the world's best, however. The Latin language itself was thought to be unsurpassed for purity, rhythmic flow and musical sound. It had a precision, a dignity, and a pithiness unknown in English or in any other language. Yet, it was capable of wide-sweeping phrases and inference; and its tone and verbal effects were magical.

Although all of this now seems to hint at snobbery, the command of a second language was basically a demonstration of learning. In the colonial era as well as the Roman age, a second language was a gauge of experience. When Caesar dined at Cicero's house, the chat was in Greek. Educated Romans, like French-speaking Russian aristocrats of the 19th Century, spoke what they considered a more cultivated tongue. Students were given another reason for studying Latin: they could thereby acquire an appreciation for Roman civilization, a well-spring of western culture. At the same time, half the English language was derived from Latin, and a real mastery of English was possible only by first mastering Latin. Finally, Latin had been the language of learning for centuries. Columbus had prepared for his voyages in Latin. Generals had used it to study tactics and strategy, merchants to keep accounts, and clerks to keep records. Latin was a gentleman's accomplishment which made the learned men of Europe one nation, in a sense, and distinguished them from the *hoi polloi* and the vulgar. Everyone who was neither a mere soldier nor craftsman wanted not just a smattering of Latin, but a living and breathing acquaintance with it—both as a spoken and a written language.

Grammar schools, therefore, gave primary attention to the poems, speeches, plays and other writings of the ancient Romans. And to master these writings, the study of *Lilly's* Latin grammar with its seven genders, 15 pages of rules and exceptions, and 25 kinds of nouns and their declensions was a prerequisite.

Grammar schools were divided into seven classes, all of which met in a single room under a single master with perhaps one assistant. Each class sat on a separate bench or "form," and the younger students in the First Form sat in front. Although they were commencing a *secondary* education which would prepare them for college, First Form students were seldom more than 7 or 8 years of age.[5]

Except for the reading of Aesop's *Fables*, which never failed to delight young boys, the first two years of grammar school education were given almost wholly to the study of grammar. First formers might study Ezekiel Cheever's *Accidence*, then move the next year in Second Form to the more difficult *Lilly's* grammar. Before age 17 or 18, by which time most boys had finished college, they had read some of the world's best literature. This included the *Annals*, an historical epic describing the founding of Rome; *Satires*, some witty observations on early Roman social life; *Georgics*, one of the most beautiful poems ever written about country living; *Metamorphoses*, a definitive reference work on mythology; *The Golden Ass*, an adventure story; *Satyricon*, western literature's first realistic novel; and *Pharsalia*, an epic poem describing the Pompey and Caesar power struggle. Boys read comedies, tragedies, philosophical works, odes, orations, biographies, and letters, all in Latin. Of this latter class, they were particularly fond of *Heroides*, a collection of fictional letters written by famous women of mythology to their dead lovers. The most universally read Latin authors were Caesar, Cicero, and Virgil. Caesar's *Commentaries* described some of his military campaigns and were written with the sure hand of genius. Cicero's *Orations* reflected the thinking of the Roman aristocracy, and showed him to be perhaps the greatest master of Latin prose. And Virgil's *Aeneid* described events leading to the creation of Rome, and was thought to be the greatest single work in all of Latin literature.

The Latin School was not a popular institution in one sense of the word. In many instances, they were set up and maintained by a small number of learned men in any given community, men who sometimes acted as an organized group to provide better education for their own children. Because they obviously constituted less than 5 per cent of the total population, these institutions clearly did not fulfill the needs of the masses. With the rising egalitarian mood that was part of the Revolutionary movement, study of a special language for the privileged few was viewed as an anachronism and, worse still, as a part of the Old World's dead hand smothering the aspirations of the New. In the words of one of the most perceptive of the new democrats, Benjamin Franklin, "most of the learning in use is of no great use." There were towns and ships to build, land to clear and cultivate, and heathen to dispossess; what was needed for a new nation were, as Franklin said, *practical* studies—mathematics, chemistry, navigation and surveying. Just as the rude marm school with its hornbook and religious cant gave way to the worldly, cultured emphases of the Latin grammar school, that institution in turn was modified to meet the needs of a new kind of community—one of variety, not stratification, and practicalities instead of moralities. That new design would be the work of enlightened school masters and aspiring communities.

Two

1 The best account by far of the early American schoolkeeper is Willard S. Elsbree, *The American Teacher* (New York: American Book Company, 1939), pp. 7-190. See also Elizabeth Porter Gould's *Ezekiel Cheever: Schoolmaster* (Boston: The Palmer Company, 1904), and Brooks, *The Oldest School*, pp. 25-40.

2 Mason S. Stone, *History of Education, State of Vermont*, (Montpelier, Capital City Press, 1936), pp. 92-92.

3 The extreme discipline used in colonial schools, and views of the child's utter depravity are described in Earle, *Child Life*, pp. 191-92; and Eggleston, *Transit of Civilization*, pp. 243-44. See also E. E. Brown, *The Making of Our Middle Schools* (New York: Longman's Green & Co., 1905), pp. 18; 49-50; 132. By "middle," Brown meant "high" schools. For related matters, see Eggleston, *Transit of Civilization*, p. 221.

4 For a variety of general works dealing with the Dutch schools of New York and other 17th Century schools still in operation, see William Heard Kirkpatrick, *The Dutch Schools of New Netherland and Colonial New York* (Washington, D. C.: U.S. Government Printing Office, 1912), p. 27. For accounts of Collegiate and Roxbury schools, still surviving, see Jean Parker Waterbury, *A History of Col-*

legiate Schools 1638-1963 (New York: Clarkson N. Potter, Inc. 1965) pp. 76-77. See also Stuart G. Noble, *A History of American Education* (New York: Rinehart & Co., 1960); Howard K. Beale, *A History of Freedom of Teaching in American Schools* (New York: Octagon Books, 1966); Vera M. Butler, *Education as Revealed by New England Newspapers* (Philadelphia: Majestic Press, 1935); and Monica Kiefer, *American Children Through Their Books 1700-1835* (Philadelphia: n.p., 1935).

[5] For excellent background on the early grammar schools in America, see Brown, *Our Middle Schools*, pp. 18-49-50, 132. See also R. F. Seybolt, *The Public Schools of Colonial Boston* (Cambridge: Harvard University Press, 1935). For the expectations of colleges and universities of the early grammar schools, see Emit. D. Grizzell, *Origin and Development of the High School in New York Before 1865* (New York: The Macmillan Company, 1923), p. 14. For the colonial curriculum, see Eggleston, *Transit of Civilization*, p. 235 and Brown, *Our Middle Schools*, p. 132. Descriptions of early backcountry grammar schools are also in Earle, *Child Life*, p. 77, and Eggleston, *Transit of Civilization*, pp. 240-41. For the grammar school rationale, see Eggleston, *Transit of Civilization*, pp. 96, 219; and Brown, *Our Middle Schools*, pp. 18, 132.

THREE
Academies for a New Republic

"His words of learned length . . .
Amazed the gazing rustics (gathered) round
And still they gazed, and still the wonder grew
That one small head could carry all he knew."

The Schoolmaster in Oliver Goldsmith's
"The Deserted Village"

Public education developed slowly during the years following the Revolutionary War. Many schools closed during that eight-year-long conflict because of financial and manpower shortages; many were destroyed in the waves of fighting that swept over every region. Moreover, the war diverted attention from training in theories to the practical skills that were needed immediately. The blessings of independence also brought with them an enormous debt, shared not only by the new confederation of states but by each community therein. Instead of being a period of stagnation, however, the leaders of the new republic used those first years to create an ideal model of education to match the other elements of their great national design.

Because education was a matter for private choice, the Founding Fathers did not include it in the matters of governmental jurisdictions defined and limited by the Constitution. But they themselves were deeply concerned with the subject as an essential element of citizenship. Among those who spoke out on questions of education as a public institution in which government at every level must be involved were Benjamin Franklin, Benjamin Rush, Samuel Knox, George Washington, John Jay and Thomas Jefferson.

29

Each of them were themselves products of the classical learning of their time, and each therefore favored particular facets of that tradition. Washington naturally urged the creation of a national university that would shape the student as citizen-soldier. Franklin characteristically called for a whole new kind of education more in keeping with revolutionary values: a break with the culture of England so widely regarded as frivolous and class-ridden.[1]

Franklin had opened an academy for learning in 1749. He based the concept on the model of Plato's school, located in an orchard owned by a war hero, Academus, near Athens. Those Englishmen such as John Milton who were so deeply impressed by Greek ideals in designing human institutions had retrieved the example. Daniel Defoe used it to designate schools wherein such specialists as linguists and musicians would reside together. In 18th Century England, about 30 specialized schools were established, each teaching classes of 20 or 30 students, subjects which grammar schools could not or would not offer: geography, higher mathematics, logic, history, anatomy and shorthand. The success of the most famous of these, Doddridge's Academy in Northhampton, opened in 1729, encouraged anti-classicists like Franklin to call for similar schools in the Colonies.

He took his own advice, set forth in a pamphlet called "A Project of an Academy." It was the design and purpose of the Greek ideal, not its linguistic and historical curriculum, that he admired. He therefore established a school in a rural setting beyond the hustle of Philadelphia, whose population of 35,000 made it the largest city in British North America and second only to London in the English-speaking world. He required his students to study not only the practical sciences of business and agriculture, but current literature as well. Moreover, they grew their own fruits, vegetables, and meats, and they swam, wrestled, and participated in track and field sports—activities heretofore unheard of in American schools. It was the founder's hope that they would above all learn the ideals of service to "mankind, country, friends and family." While Franklin believed that the purpose of education was to train youth to "serve the public with honor" to themselves and to their country, he also thought it

30

should prepare them for successful careers and good character. Although he thought less of music, art and dancing, those subjects were taught at his school as well. Intending to avoid the customary cant and squabbling about religion, he established a non-denominational board of trustees. Eventually, however, they overruled his desire to dispense with the English curriculum entirely.[2]

The idea of the academy was modified in the midst of the Revolutionary War by a man who shared Franklin's pragmatism: Judge Samuel Phillips of Andover, Massachusetts. As a descendant of the first families of Boston, he had every reason to be conservative. Instead, he wrote

> our general plan of educating youth is injudicious, unnatural and absurd. As soon as an infant is capable of muttering English, he is put to his accidence. In the Latin, youth fall back upon something that has been dead these hundred years and will never exist again, but if there were not a fragment of the language remaining, it would not exclude us from heaven. In it they study months without one new idea, and yet it has a great tendency to make the little ignorant scholar a pedant, if he can throw out one Latin word, though he knows no more of its signification than a parrot. The Latin authors were pagans, and their works all contain more or less of the foolishness and stupid religion of their times. I think they ought not to be read until a person is established in our pure and holy religion. It is a pity that the best six years of youth should be spent in studying heathen writers.[3]

Phillips founded the academy bearing his name in 1778; three years later, his Uncle John founded a second Phillips Academy in Exeter, New Hampshire, 30 miles away. (Today, they are thought to be among the best secondary schools in the world.)

The spokesman for the Revolutionary generation, Thomas Jefferson, was an aristocrat who advocated a political and social system completely opposed to his own class. Although inclined to the Greek classical tradition in many of

31

his interests, his educational philosophy reflected the writings of Jean Jacques Rousseau, the French philosopher who believed that education should encourage self-expression rather than impose discipline. While the American revolutionaries had followed the precepts of that Age of Reason, their admirers in France observed that human justice could also be bound by mere reason. Their revolution would embody Rousseau's emphasis on emotion, spontaneity, and natural growth.

Jefferson advocated schools for all boys and all girls, and a free secondary education for talented indigent boys, the best of whom could then move on to a free university education, then serve their government for a stipulated period after graduation. Those not bright enough for a university education could become teachers, Jefferson believed. He proposed a university for his state of Virginia and submitted a design for the campus buildings which still stand at its center. Jefferson also designed the ordinances enacted by Congress in 1785 and 1787 which reserved a section of land in each township division of the nation's public domain, the sale of which was to be used for building educational facilities. Although the reserves had slight value at the time, the great movement of population into the trans-Mississippi West subsequently proved the importance of those provisions. Not only did they establish education as a proper and natural part of governmental institutions, the ordinances were precedents for the allocation of public funds for education.[4]

The changeover to academics was not abrupt, but was accomplished by a gradual broadening of the curriculum of the Latin grammar schools. Many kinds of institutions became academies in nature, if not in name. Generally, academies were incorporated, non-profit, non-denominational, privately managed secondary schools, although one or more of those elements might be missing in schools that were academies as well. In the words of Noah Webster, they constituted an "Americanization" of education. They boarded their students, making them part of the region itself, and prepared them for "all things useful *and* ornamental." A comparison of the curriculums of the classical and English courses offered at a New England academy in 1818 shows the advantages—and attractiveness—of such studies:

ENGLISH	CLASSICAL
1st Year. English grammar, reading, punctuation, geography, arithmetic, algebra.	**1st Year.** Adams' *Latin Grammar*, Liber Primus, Caesar's *Commentaries*, Prosody, geography, Virgil, arithmetic.
2nd. Year. English grammar, geometry, trigonometry, mensuration, history, logic, rhetoric, English composition, declamation.	**2nd. Year.** Virgil, arithmetic, Valpey's Greek grammar, Roman history, Cicero's *Orations*, Delectus, Greek Testament, English grammar, declamation.
3rd. Year Surveying, navigation, chemistry, natural philosophy, modern history English composition, forensics, and declamation.	**3rd. Year.** Latin & Greek authors in revision; English grammar and declamation, Sallust, Algebra, Latin and English translations and composition.[5]

While Latin grammar schools had been local institutions catering to those who lived close by, academies were more regional in their appeal and influence. Generally, they were boarding schools, and they offered students a wider choice of subjects than had been available at the grammar schools. Boys *and* girls—though mostly boys—studied as "English" students (non-college bound) and as Latin students (college bound). Something of a pecking order developed among students along curricular lines. Those who studied the English curriculum were jealous and contemptuous of their "elitist" fellows who studied the classics; and Latin students despaired of the philistines who were not college bound. Still, there was great fun and competition between the two groups. On a given night, to break monotony or just to vent their spleen, Latin students might salt the water well at the English dormitory. The next night, to pay them back, the English students might stuff obstructions down the Latin dormitory chimney, smoking the classicists out into the snow.

The routine for Latin students at the academies was much the same as at the old grammar schools. A school often consisted of 50 or 60 students, divided into different classes or forms. They often met in small, one-room buildings and studied under a single teacher. The day commenced only after a reading from the Bible, a hymn and a prayer. Usually, the teacher began with the lowest class and worked up—as one form recited, the others prepared for their own recitations. The master called on specific students to "parse" a word, or describe it grammatically telling its part of speech, inflectional form and syntactic relations. Others "construed" or told the meaning and intention of the word. Moving to the next class, the master listened to a few students read stories from Aesop's *Fables*. By lunch time, he had moved through all the forms. After lunch, the entire school wrote Latin, but the more advanced of them might also parse and construe 100 or 150 lines from Virgil and then be examined in prosody and Latin prose. At the end of the day, devotions were said, and boys scrambled to their dormitories for supper.

There were increased demands for schooling from women and from workers during the academy period, and two experiments resulted. These demands were a part of the same egalitarian trend that had culminated in the American Revolution, and they posed logistical problems that are familiar in our own time: how could large numbers of students be taught with a short supply of teachers? Two solutions were offered. One called for use of a "Lancastrian" system of schooling, by which a single teacher and 30 or 40 student assistants could teach up to five hundred students at a time. The other called for adding teacher-preparatory courses to the academy curriculum, thereby attracting large numbers of future teachers. (Classical graduates seldom went into teaching.) Both schemes were tried, and both failed.

The first had been devised in 1801 by an English educator named Joseph Lancaster. His idea was a system of mutual instruction by which the older and better students helped in the teaching of the younger and less able. The key to the scheme was the use of an elaborate system of bells, whistles, hand signals and verbal commands designed to minimize confusion and create something of a martial atmosphere in the classroom. The teaching of an algebra problem illustrates the Lancastrian scheme, by which thousands of early American children were taught. First, the attention of students was fixed with the command, "PREPARE." When order had been obtained, the command was given, "FIND 'X' IF _____." Students worked at their desks until a third command, "HANDS BEHIND," was given. Then assistants moved through the room helping students and making corrections. Then came the order, "CLEAN SLATES," and another problem was presented in like manner. Even the dismissal of students at the end of the day came in eight military-like steps. "LOOK" was a preparatory command to fix attention. At the commands "OUT" and "FRONT," students rose from their seats and faced the teacher. At the command "TAKE HATS," "HATS ON," and "HANDS DOWN," they located their hats, raised them to their heads, and lowered their hands to their sides. Finally, at the command, "LOOK," the instructor indicated the desired exit, and at the command "GO," students filed quietly out of the building.

Needless to say, the scheme was never popular. It was cheap, it was relatively efficient, and it even seemed for a while to be the answer to many of the problems of educating the new masses. But students didn't like it. They abhorred its impersonalization, and they dreaded the regimentation and the tedium and unnaturalness of it all. Lancaster was pronounced a fraud and a charlatan, and after a decade or so the scheme was abandoned altogether.[6]

Phillips Academy at Andover was the first to add a teacher training course to its curriculum. Other academies followed suit, and ultimately thousands of teachers were attracted to their teacher programs and into the budding teaching profession. Subsequently, normal schools and then colleges and universities assumed this role. But in the 19th Century, a secondary education ending at age 14 or 15 was more than adequate training for school masters, and indeed this idea persisted even into the 20th Century. Attempts to upgrade teaching and produce a larger supply of teachers were begun at Phillips Academy in 1830. "The most prominent object" of that new program, the school's catalog pointed out, was to "educate instructers (sic) of common and other schools." To bring this about, Samuel Hall, who seven years earlier had established the first normal school in the country, was retained as school principal. Hall had also written the first textbook on teaching which he titled *Lectures On Schoolkeeping*. During his years at the academy, enrollment tripled and facilities were improved. In addition to his course on schoolkeeping, Hall taught mathematics, geography, grammar, history, composition, drawing, music, philosophy, chemistry and political science. He also established the first laboratory teaching school in the country while at the academy.[7]

But the idea of training teachers at academies never really caught on. The classical faculties and students never accepted the weaker and below-the-mark students whom teaching attracted. There were endless squabbles between them, and the "careerists" usually lost. So great were the disputes, in fact, and so numerous were the complaints that teachers lowered the prestige of academies, that the idea of normal schools, where teacher candidates prepared themselves in isolation from the more academically minded students, began to take strong hold. Indeed, just as academies all over the country began to drop their teacher training programs, Horace Mann opened the first American normal school in Massachusetts, and the trend toward state-supported normal schools was then set. Academies had very much needed the teacher programs to stem their sinking enrollments; the classicist-careerist relationship had been much more symbiotic than either of the parties had imagined. The departure of teachers finally helped seal the academy's fate.

If the grammar schools had too much emphasized the imminence of death—"while youth do cheer, death may be near"—the academies emphasized, in the words of one of the many founders, "the great end and real business of *living*." (Emphasis added). It was not the job of academies to confound the "oulde deluder Satan" by preparing the young for *death*, but in fact, just the opposite—to prepare the young for *life*. This "preparation for life" idea permeates the whole of academy literature. The grim solemnities of the early school began to give way to the optimism of the academy. The religious spirit was there at the academies; sometimes it was strong; but it began to dwindle and fade, and denominationalists became interested in education for its own sake.

Although academies were secondary schools, they were attended by students of all ages. Many were only 7 or 8 years old, and as many others were in their late teens or early twenties. The age of many in the lower classes often exceeded the average age of those in the highest class. Not only were they different in age, but they came from widely differing backgrounds, and they were bound for widely differing careers—the pulpit, the bank, the bar, the farm or the classroom, a different situation indeed from the old days when most students had been bound for the ministry.[8]

The most prestigious academies were in New England, and they attracted the children of many of America's great families. Nine of George Washington's relatives attended Phillips at Andover, for example, as did such New England old-liners as the Wendells, the Holmeses, the Beechers and the Stowes, and the Waldos, Emersons, Quincys, Adamses, Lowells and Lodges. Others, such as John C. Calhoun, attended prestigious Southern schools such as South Carolina's Waddel Academy, and were able to move smoothly from such schools into their junior years at Yale or Harvard.

But for every prestigious school for the well-to-do, there were hundreds, perhaps even thousands of academies for students of more average means. In 1855, at the height of the academy period, educator Henry Barnard counted more than 6,000 academies in operation with a total enrollment exceeding 250,000. Many of these institutions were chartered, heavily-endowed and long-lived, and they offered excellent teachers and courses. But as many others were pretentious, one-teacher operations offering, incredibly, upward of 50 to 70 subjects per term. Many of these schools scrimped by financially, and their instruction and facilities were marginal at best. Tuition, their life's blood, was negotiable—and as was the case in the old days, students paid their fees in firewood, farm labor, kitchen staples, farm equipment or draft animals. Home-canned fruits and vegetables, rarities at the time, were welcomed in lieu of tuition. But many other schools were merely hopeful. One 19th Century school made no bones about its admissions policies, and declared openly in its catalog: "too many people have a wrong idea as to who is eligible for admission here. They think that only those well qualified can enter; but actually, we accept students of all grades of advancement." There were academies for every segment and stratum of society, and the majority of schools admitted virtually anyone who could pay, barter or beg his way through the schoolhouse door.[9]

Student life vastly diversified during the Academy period. Now, there was no reason not to have a little fun to coat the bitter pill of learning, and social fraternities began to spring up everywhere. Baseball and football were introduced on American campuses, although football was loudly railed against as "disgraceful to those of refinement and better education." By the 1870's, many schools had begun to celebrate Christmas, and even to give a two or three day holiday to mark the occasion. Most New England faculties objected, however, on the grounds that a "festival" atmosphere developed, and students took to revelry, dancing and drink.[10]

School discipline took a turn for the better during the Academy period, reflecting the work of Rousseau's disciple, Johann Pestalozzi. In 1800, he had opened a school modeled on Rousseau's theories at Yverodon in Switzerland, and many of his ideas made their way to American campuses. Chiefly, this was the work of educator John Griscom of New York who had visited these schools in Europe in 1818, and then published his account of them in *A Year In Europe*, one of the most influential educational works of the 19th Century.[11] It was this book that called into question the harsh disciplinary measures that heretofore had characterized the American School. The insistence of Rousseau and Pestalozzi on schooling in harmony with the nature of the child, and on teacher training, helped to pave the way toward open and less authoritarian education in the nation's schools. On the whole, the discipline in the academies was much milder than that of the grammar schools, but then the student body was somewhat more mature in thought, behavior and purpose.

The quasi-public character of academy financing was another of its distinguishing features, and it showed a tentative but slowly growing popular commitment in the country toward education. Most 19th Century Americans favored schools, but only to a point. They objected to being taxed to pay for them. They were much more willing, in fact, to grant a school a charter and perhaps an initial grant of money or land than to offer full-time financial support. The idea was to "encourage" schools, to grant them sporadic aid, and even to help bail them out when they got into trouble. But most people were not willing to go beyond that. States did not found academies, and they did not require counties or towns to do so. They did, however, encourage private initiatives. If a group of men could obtain a building and a small faculty, and attract enough tuition-paying students to offer a hope of success, then a state or county or town might bring together some financial help. Or they might put the schools in the way to make some money of their own through various lottery schemes or through managing or renting out public property or lands. Sometimes towns turned over fine or penalty income for the support of a school, or leased a public building to a school at a reduced rate. These indirect encouragements could go only so far, though, and academies actually succeeded only to the degree to which they attracted cash-paying students.

A student's fees depended not only on the number of subjects taken but on their "respectability." Classical studies had a better reputation, and they cost more, even though the demand for them came to be less than that for English studies. Another factor was probably at work here in that those most able to pay were also most likely to opt for the classical curriculum. Only rarely did states seek any degree of control over the academies within their jurisdiction. Except for New York, their private governance and operation was virtually complete.

Significantly, the age of the academy coincided with the beginnings of the movement to recognize women's rights. In the wake of the Industrial Revolution it the early 19th Century, feudal sex roles began to change, and women became gradually more assertive in their bids for voting rights and education. Indeed, the education of women may be cited as one of the academy's most important contributions to the national coming-of-age. The humanizing influence of women, many of whom had been "humanized" at academies, is seen in all the important social movements of the 19th Century, especially in temperance and education reform, the abolition of slavery, and the advocacy of religious liberalism. This theme is further discussed in Chapter 7.

If academies were successful regarding women, they were usually unsuccessful in their attempts to upgrade teacher ranks. According to contemporary assessments, far from being an educated elite, the average teacher was a poorly educated transient who moved from job to job, unable to make a go of any of them. On rare occasions, a teacher of refinement, culture and erudition could be found, but such qualities usually were missing. Many teachers of the period were "of the adventurous type, migratory, odd in habits, and frequently questionable in conduct." As a class they were "generally loose and immoral," and they lacked even a smattering of professional standards or pride. Not only were these teachers unable to inspire confidence in schools, they usually brought education into public contempt and retarded its growth. One state governor complained that they were "ignorant and possessed of an easy morality," and a college president of the period wrote that a great number of teachers were "lazy, drunken, unprincipled vagabonds" who were also "alcoholics, thieves, sadists and plain ignoramusses."[12] Of course, there were also many excellent teachers during the academy period. Eliphalet Pearson (whose students called him "Elephant" because of his great size) was a botanist, ornithologist, musician, writer, farmer, businessman and linguist. His friend George Washington said of Pearson that he was capable "not only to lead boys, but to command men." Oliver Wendell Holmes immortalized the brilliant, talented and inspiring "Elephant" in his poem, "The School Boy." Ebenezer Pemberton was another exceptional teacher, who had stood to inherit a fortune had he only agreed to give up teaching for the pulpit.

40

Among "his boys" were Aaron Burr, James Madison, Charles Pinckney Sumner, Stephen Longfellow, and Charles Lowell. And Osgood Johnson was one of the great teachers of the academy period. His students remembered his "intellectual keenness, unsullied ideals, and magnetic presence." A genius whose active mind literally burned out his frail body, Johnson died at the age of 34. He was a searching and thorough scholar, and he lectured entirely without notes.[13]

The academy's decline was undoubtedly caused by the high school's spectacular rise, as the following statistics indicate. These refer to New York State, but the general trends were similar in all states.[14]

| | NUMBER | | ENROLLMENT | |
	Academies	High Schools	Academies	High Schools
1865	165	35	29,423	6,710
1870	115	67	19,717	10,596
1875	97	119	15,932	14,222
1880	82	155	12,116	18,983
1885	71	190	12,265	24,778

The academy cultivated a new nationalism not only through instruction in American history, but through "Americanizing" spelling, textbooks, and the general school environment; it opened the door, however slightly, to the co-education of the sexes, admitting a very few girls, but nonetheless putting girls on a more or less equal standing with boys, while purging from courses and textbooks (particularly those in anatomy) anything to bring a blush to a delicate cheek. It did continue to teach girls, however, that their true role was to make their classic limitations work in their favor; and that to really win in their competition with boys, they did so only by "losing." The academy also bridged the passage from ecclesiastical schools to secular education, depending as it did for financial support from all quarters, whatever their religious beliefs. And finally, the academy

41

began very slowly to throw out the old classical curriculum and all that had been considered "knowledge" for centuries. But tradition was strong, and Latin and the classics were to coexist with and often eclipse English studies right up to the present century.[15]

Altered political and economic conditions of the new country had called for a different kind of school than that which had suited a stratified colonial society and a thinly spread population. The academy had been the answer. But by 1860 an increased segment of the nation's population lived in cities, most of them founded since the end of the Revolution. Urbanization made town and city day schools more practical than the rural academies. And the egalitarian tide which had helped to usher in the Revolution was deepening. A new and more democratic school—a truly free one—was now called for.

Three

[1] John Allen Kront and Dixon Ryan Fox, *The Completion of Independence: 1790-1830* (New York: The Macmillan Co., 1944), p. 132. See also Russel Blaine Nye's *Cultural Life of the New Nation: 1776-1830* (New York: Harper & Row Publishers, 1960), pp. 124-29.

[2] Merle Curti, *The Social Ideas of American Educators*, (New York: Charles Scribner's Sons, 1935), pp. 34-40. See also Thomas Woody, *Educational Views of Benjamin Franklin* (New York: McGraw-Hill, Inc., 1931).

[3] Quoted in C. M. Fuess, *An Old New England School* (Boston: Houghton Mifflin Co., 1917), pp. 58-59.

[4] Roy J. Honeywell, *The Educational Work of Thomas Jefferson*, (Cambridge: Harvard University Press, 1931) p. 159. See also James B. Conant, *Thomas Jefferson and the Development of American Public Education*, (Berkeley: University of California Press, 1962), p. 3.

[5] E. E. Brown, *Our Middle Schools*, pp. 327-38.

[6] Jean Parker Waterbury, *A History of Collegiate School, 1638-1963*, (New York: Clarkson N. Potter, Inc., 1965), pp. 74-79. In addition to the U.S., England, France and Germany, the Lancastrian scheme was tried in several

South American countries. See David Salmon's *Joseph Lancaster* (London: Longman's Green & Co., Ltd., 1904), and Lancaster's own book, *The Lancastrian System of Education, With Improvements*, published by the author, Baltimore, 1821.

[7] Fuess, *An Old New England School*, p. 209 Hall's book of 13 lectures still makes interesting reading. See Samuel Read Hall, *Lectures On School Keeping*, eds. Arthur Wright and George Gardner (Boston: Richardson, Lord and Holbrook, 1829; reprinted ed., n.p. Dartmouth Press, 1929).

[8] Nye, *Cultural Life Of the New Nation*, p. 164. See also G. F. Miller, *The Academy System of the State of New York* (New York: Columbia University Press, 1922, reprint ed., New York: Arno Press, 1969), pp. 35-37.

[9] Theodore Sizer, *The Age of Academies* (Richmond, Va: William Byrd Press, 1964), p. 38.

[10] Fuess, *An Old New England School*, p. 291. See also Foster Rhea Dulles, *America Learns to Play*, (New York: n.p., 1940), pp. 67-79, 136-45.

[11] Nye, *Cultural Life of the New Nation*, pp. 166-67. Griscom's *A Year in Europe* was reviewed in the *North American Review*, January, 1824. See also Brown, *Our Middle Schools*, p. 244.

[12] Sizer, *Age of Academies*, p. 21. See also Edgar W. Knight, *Public Education in the South*, (Boston: n.p., 1922), pp. 294-95. See also Knight's *A Documentary History of Education in the South Before 1860* (Chapel Hill: University of North Carolina Press, 1949), pp. 5, 231. See also Sizer, *Age of Academies*, p. 39, and Nye, *Cultural Life of the New Nation*, p. 163.

[13] Fuess, *An Old New England School*, p. 209.

[14] Miller, *Academy System of New York*, p. 53.

[15] Military academies, although of a different breed from those under discussion, were established all over the country during the 19th Century, and they were particularly evident in the South. Usually, they were really state munitions garrisons which were manned by academy students. General William T. Sherman was Principal of such a school in Louisiana, but resigned to rejoin the U.S. Army just before the Civil War. His academy became Louisiana State

University, just as Franklin's academy became the University of Pennsylvania. The U.S. Military and Naval academies were established in 1802 and 1845, and after slow starts (particularly at West Point) went on to become outstanding schools.

FOUR
The Labors of Two Heroes

"Mann come (sic) yesterday to resign his tutorial dignities."

**A student's comment on
Horace Mann's resignation from
his first teaching job, 1821.**[1]

Historians have called the period from the 1820's to the 1850's the Age of Reform and the Age of the Common Man. In those years, fundamental changes occurred in the status of women, workers and blacks; ballots were won for the non-propertied; prison sentences for indebtedness were abolished; and much was done to curb alcohol abuse, and the exploitation of children who commonly worked 16-hour days for $1.25 per week. All of these reform movements were connected; they were the warp and woof of a general reform fabric. None existed independently of the other, and it is impossible to judge where one began and another left off. Almost universally, however, the educational reform movement was thought to be central to the success of each of the other movements.[2]

But generations of Americans living in that period held apparently contradictory views about education. They believed that any man could attain any kind of success through the exercise of his own talents. With but a few months of education, their hero, Andrew Jackson, had been a schoolmaster at age 15, had defeated Indian armies and Wellington's veterans, had built three Hermitages, had been elevated to presidential candidacy by the acclaim of citizens in every part of the United States, and had ultimately presided over a prospering nation during two terms in office. There were similar heroes in every region, and they had similar successes. At the same time, astounding economic and social expansion was the work of technicians and professionals, men who mastered the practicalities of building trade routes and cities, and supplying the increasing populations using them. Their know-how had seemed to spring from an educational basis.

The increasing needs for such practical skills prepared the way for public support of such an educational basis. But in this matter, as in every other field of growth during that expansive age, that public understanding was brought about by the efforts of heroes. Horace Mann and Henry Barnard were both New Englanders. That region's 200-year tradition of support for free public elementary (common) schools, had not, however, produced excellence in any aspect of education. Most school buildings were inadequately built and equipped, and many were unfit for occupancy. Compulsory attendance laws were not enforced, and thousands of children worked 90-hour weeks in mills and factories. At the heart of such problems was a pinch-penny, apathetic tax-paying public.

Like so many of his contemporaries, Horace Mann rose above such conditions. His education in a Massachusetts rural school had been so poor that his mother was obliged to hire an itinerant schoolmaster to tutor him for Brown University's entrance examination. In Mann's recollection, that teacher was often "too drunk to teach." But he was a brilliant classicist—he had committed most of Virgil to memory—and he was able to coach young Mann to a passing score on the examination. Once admitted to the Rhode Island university, Mann compiled a brilliant record and was elected valedictorian of the 1819 graduating class.[3] Afterward, Mann taught for two years, but students disliked him almost from the beginning. He was rather overbearing at that age; he was glib and bitingly sarcastic; he lorded it over his students at every turn; he dressed like a "dandy" and strutted back and forth in his classroom pontificating on every subject; and he gave students low marks and outrageously difficult assignments as if to point up their many weaknesses and his own strengths. When they had finally had enough of him, they hooted and hollered him from the classroom. When he later resigned, one student wrote (without a trace of regret) that Mann had "resigned his tutorial dignities." Once free of the tensions of teaching, Mann blossomed. His undergraduate record at Brown won him a seat at Judge Tapping Reeve's law school in Litchfield, Connecticut. This one-room, white frame school, which sat in the back yard of the judge's home (and which still stands today) was the first law school in the United States. (It was established in 1784; Aaron Burr had been the school's first student, and John C. Calhoun and three future Supreme Court justices would also study there). Mann excelled in his studies at Litchfield. He matured "beyond measure" from his teaching days, and he became one of the best-read and most popular students at the school; he was acknowledged to be a "fast-study," the brightest student in school. Moreover, he was tall, handsome, "intolerably witty," one student remembered, and he was widely sought out at parties and social functions for his glibness and gifts for conversation and repartee. He was an immaculate dresser, and was remembered by a number of girls who attended a nearby "female seminary" as being a "charmer," much given to wine, card games and good cigars.

After graduation, Mann moved to Boston and set up a law practice. During the next few years, he married the daughter of the president of his alma mater, built up a first-rate law practice, and accumulated a sizable fortune from lending money and manufacturing. He moved easily among the Boston elite, and at age 31 was elected to the state legislature. Swept up by the climate of human and institutional reform of that time, he actively supported the establishment of the first state hospital for "lunatics and persons furiously mad" in the United States. He was on his way to becoming governor of Massachusetts, it was widely acknowledged, and it was assumed that he then could have any national office he wanted. But then tragedy struck, and Mann would never be the same again, His young and much-loved wife died. Increasingly, throughout the 1830's, he drew inward. He became an ascetic. Preferring solitude, he dropped out of Boston's social whirl. He became more and more morose and depressed. He neglected his law practice and other businesses. He began to think of suicide, and he wondered aloud in his diary how much longer he was "doomed to live." "When, oh when, will this life cease," he wrote. He began to hallucinate, writing again in his diary that he felt himself being "carried away by demons to the centre of universal darkness." Mann became, in effect, something of a tormented genius. By 1837, he was at the end of his tether. He had begun to move, he wrote in his diary, in a "world of shadows and gloomy images." Physically and emotionally, he had sunk to his lowest ebb.

Then, in 1837, his friends in the Massachusetts Legislature established a 10-member State Board of Education, the first of its kind in the country, and invited Mann to become its first salaried executive and secretary. The pay was a pittance, and the work—riding horseback all over the state documenting the condition of Massachusetts schools— would be grueling. Moreover, it was an advisory position only; it carried with it no power or opportunities to exercise initiatives. It meant a lot of "privation, labor and infinite annoyance from an infinite number of schemers," Mann wrote. Yet, there was also a chance to do much good, he believed, seeing more to the low-level, innocuous job than anyone else at the time. Indeed, Mann wrote in his diary, here was a chance to do "glorious deeds," to do work that would improve the lives of the "multitudes." He took the job, and wrote in his diary that he was abandoning law for what he saw as the "larger spheres of minds and morals." Henceforth, he wrote in the sure language of a visionary, "as long as I hold this office, I devote myself to the supermost welfare of mankind upon the earth." Perhaps only visionaries see opportunities to serve "mankind" in such trifling, bureaucratic work as the job accepted by Mann.[4]

Mann took up his new mission with appropriate zeal. He announced the formation of the new State Board of Education, and the forthcoming county conventions it would sponsor. He himself made plans to visit every county and hundreds of schools throughout the state. Massachusetts schools were the best in the country, it was widely acknowledged, and if they were bad, as only he suspected (doubtless

48

because of his problems years earlier in getting into Brown University), then the schools of the entire country were in even worse shape. He sent letters to friends all over the state suggesting how they might promote better schools in their own communities. He read widely in order to determine what might be the best new roads to take in the areas of school building construction, textbooks and curricula. He gave support to any organization or political group which could help with his work, among these the American Institute of Instruction; and he began to reorganize local common school improvement associations. Then he began to secure from leading local citizens—ministers, newspaper editors and businessmen—endorsements for the work he was about to undertake.

In 1838, Mann rode circuit for two months. In dawn-to dusk, 20-mile-per-day rides, he traveled through western Massachusetts visiting schools and talking with local officials. He spoke to every audience he could gather. Public schools, he told them, were a necessary foundation for democracy; they were "equalizers" and creators of wealth, and they were an untapped resource for the moral and civic training of youth. To the poor, he promised that education was a means for acquiring property; to the rich, he emphasized that only the educated would respect property. By doubling his Saturday rides to 40 miles to avoid Sunday travel (which custom forbade though his own religious views did not), he traveled more than 500 miles, an enormous distance considering that many of the roads he traveled were little more than pig trails. But the fatiguing and wearisome work, which even wore out Mann's horse, was therapeutic for him. The bouts of despondency that had altered his youthful demeanor after the death of his wife (and business reverses and problems with his brother) now became less frequent and less severe. After only a few weeks on his new mission he wrote his sister: "I confess I feel now more as though life had a value, and as though I had a specific work to do."

Mann's circuit trip had been a revelation. He found the most deplorable conditions in the very schools which were thought to be the best in the nation. As many as 15 children were often crowded into a 14-by-18 foot space; equipment beyond the standard stove, a few tables and benches, and a water pail and dipper were almost non-existent; and many schools, both town and country, lacked even a water well or the amenity of an outhouse. His survey of more than 500 Essex County schoolhouses revealed that in those particulars which contribute to even the most basic comforts and conveniences of life, convicts at the state prison were better provided for than the children of Massachusetts. The average worth of a New England schoolhouse (in 1980 dollars) was somewhat less than $200. He found a hopeless "textbook" situation—each child providing his own when and if circumstances permitted. In one small school, Mann found 15 geography books and eight grammar books, all of comparable difficulty, but all produced by different authors and publishers. Free and uniform textbooks were unheard of, indeed, unwanted, since parents were suspicious of what the state might have their children read. He also learned with little surprise that men teachers were paid $15 per month, and women half as much. As a result, that profession was crowded with the very dregs, the down-and-outers of society. Exceptions like the young Henry Thoreau and Herman Melville, who taught at Concord and Pittsfield, soon quit in disgust—Thoreau after only two weeks on the job, and Melville after four months.

At the heart of the dilemma of poor schoolhouses and poor teachers was the attitude of many parents that schools were a waste of time so far as the real business of earning a living was concerned. They believed that a few winter terms at a district school were quite enough education for those who would only farm or work in the factories anyway. The wealthy were often as distrustful of schools as the poor. Some of the state's most prominent citizens had nothing but contempt for Mann and his work to lift up the masses. One attorney told him that the primary duty of the privileged was to "prevent ingress" into the ranks of the privileged by the riff-raff. Reflecting a climate of opinion in which Social Darwinism would soon flourish, many believed that the condition of most of mankind was the working of immutable laws of nature; that is, that most people were destined to live in vulgar circumstances, while a few, by virtue of their birth and position, were destined sternly to guide or benevolently lead the ignorant masses. Some of New England's gentry branded Mann as just another demagogue reformer exploiting the weak and downtrodden for their votes. Indeed, it was an ironic coalition of the ignorant and the well-educated that opposed Mann at every turn and did all in their power to obstruct educational reform.

When he delivered his first annual report to the State Board of Education in 1838, Mann had inspected—and he knew firsthand—the condition of more than 1,000 Massachusetts schools. His intimate knowledge of their almost unbelievable limitations, and his factual, scientifically unemotional presentation quickly convinced the Board that despite the claims of politicians, the state had not conscientiously supported schools for the past 200 years, but indeed had neglected them with almost total disregard. The "best" schools in the country, so long New England's pride, were in fact an abomination. Indifference and carelessness had left them in a shameful state. Although politicians had boasted for generations about the state's model schools, such accounts had only been political bluster. The Board encouraged former Senator Mann to translate his findings into remedial legislation. Mann submitted a steady stream of proposals, and in doing so, became one of the first educational lobbyists in history. Like his many successors in that role, he called for better administrative and financial support of schools. Some communities, he pointed out, kept 16-week school terms, and others only four or fewer; some spent $5 per child *per annum* on education, and some spent only a few cents. He also spoke out against competing private academies, the educational establishment of the day, saying that they hindered the growth of education for the masses, and that *public* schools could do a better job of educating children anyway. He called for better school boards (pay members if necessary, he said); he called for the consolidation of literally thousands of small schools into larger and better schools, having found on his circuit ride eight schools within walking distance of a single small town. Schools should have playgrounds, water wells, wood sheds, outhouses and clocks, he said. They should keep attendance and financial records, and submit these to the state board each year. Drawing upon his earlier experience in the senate, he secured the appointment of legislators friendly to his programs as members of important legislative committees. He personally urged them to support revision of the state's fragmented education code. That statute consisted of more than 70 sections and dealt with everything from teacher certification requirements to a requirement that college students pay cash for their beer. He called for free and standardized textbooks.

Mann also raised money from private sources to help establish teacher training or "normal" schools, that word deriving from the Latin noun *norma*, meaning rule, pattern or model. (Hence, a normal school was where one learned the rules or the "how-to's" of teaching). He also had draftsmen draw plans for three model school buildings, all providing generous space, lighting, seating and ventilation, and distributed these plans to more than 6,000 school districts with the suggestion that many of the old structures be abandoned, and new structures built. By doing so he brought about the construction of hundreds of new school buildings in the state.

Mann's first year was an impressive achievement: as he jubilantly wrote to a friend, all of his recommendations were turned into law. But more importantly, he had captured the imagination of people all over the state; he had fired them up, and got them talking about and working to improve the condition of the state's schools. Moreover, he was beginning to attract the attention of social and political leaders, not only in other parts of the country, but around the world.[5]

Mann's most significant achievement was to set the machinery in motion to replace the private academy with the public high school, the term "high school" being copied from the name Edinburgh, Scotland, had given its secondary school, the "Royal High School," which was founded in the 1500's. The first American high school, however, was called the "English Classical School," meaning that it offered both an "English" and a "Latin" course of study. The school was founded in Boston in 1821. To get into this school, students had to know the three R's and be at least 12 years of age. In the course of three years, they studied English grammar, speech, literature, mathematics, navigation, surveying, geography, history and ethics. (Perhaps as a comment on the glaring lack in our own times, it should be noted that students were spared the trauma of foreign languages). High schools experienced slow growth initially against the still-prestigious academy. Moreover, with the coming of the high school (which was indigenous to the U.S.), the grammar school (which was indigenous to Europe, and which originally was aristocratic and exclusive), took on a new shape and form. Now, the grammar school became an elementary school, and high schools came to be seen as an extension of these grammar or elementary schools.

The real significance of Mann's life and work is that he established a social and political base for public education. He did this under the most difficult of conditions, during the very heyday of private academies, when most leaders were declaring that it would be suicidal to lavish state resources on public schools since the existing private academies offered better instruction, required almost no tax support, and were "better adjusted to the character, habits, and wants of the country."

Mann made a second important contribution while serving as secretary of the State Board of Education. Twelve annual reports were published which became hallmarks of American educational literature. He also published the *Common School Journal*, (Massachusetts), and in this journal and in his many lectures across the country, he fought sectarianism in schools and condemned its chief proponent, the American Sunday School Union. Similarly, he fought entrenched conservatism in the ranks of teachers, especially fomented by the Association of Masters of the Boston Public Schools, the members of which he pointedly nicknamed the "Boston birchmen." He traveled widely in Europe and studied many different kinds of schools with a view to molding the ideal American school of the future. He advocated the phonic method of teaching reading, and, significantly, he helped end a two-century tradition of oppressive student discipline. So comprehensive and fundamental were Mann's reforms that his work was copied in every section of the country, including the South immediately after the Civil War. Educators in Argentina and Chile and in many other parts of the world worked to bring about in their own countries the same reforms that Mann had won in the United States.

While privately considering his life and career "more death than life," his enemies unintentionally marked the strength of his efforts by vainly seeking to abolish his job. Mann's replacement, Barnas Sears, would later extend his reform movement into the South. This theme is further discussed in Chapter 5.

Concluding that the issue of slavery had come to "precede and outrank even education itself," Mann left his educational post to replace the late John Quincy Adams in the U.S. House of Representatives. There, he joined the growing ranks of those determined to put an end to slavery in the United States once and for all. Regretably, he did not live to see either his educational efforts or his fight against slavery brought to their final conclusion. But long before the end of his life he had happily remarried, and had ceased to wonder gloomily if his life had not been "more death than life," or if he was "doomed to live much longer." In one of his last speeches, given just a few weeks before his death, he told a weeping audience of friends that he would give anything to have one more lifetime before him; if he had he would enroll himself anew "in a 50-years' campaign, and fight once more for the glory of God and the happiness of humanity."[6] But for Horace Mann, a tormented genius with a deep-rooted instinct for creation, and blind to all except some disturbing vision in his soul, the very history of this country would be vastly different.

His contemporary, Henry Barnard of Connecticut, was an unabashed supporter of the *status quo*—in all but education. Indeed, his educational experiences constituted a cross-section of American schooling in the first half of the 19th Century. In an amazing similarity to Mann, Barnard had excelled in college despite a "miserable" district school background, taught school just as briefly, and then studied law. He too was elected to his state legislature, and there helped obtain passage of a law establishing a State Board of

Education. Barnard then became secretary of the State Board at age 27, and took up the same duties as had been prescribed from Mann the previous year in neighboring Massachusetts. Barnard's subsequent study of conditions in the Connecticut district schools, for which he was paid $3 per day, confirmed that they had "sunk into a deplorable state." Not one family in a hundred, he reported, relied upon district schools for the education of their children. Moreover, more money was spent on the private education of 12,000 students than on almost 60,000 who attended public schools. Only slightly more than half the state's children between 6 and 16 attended school with any regularity, and 8,000 did not attend at all. He chose the same means that Mann was using. In more than 400 visits to schools around the state, and in more than 100 meetings, with every school organization in Connecticut, he spoke out for better school buildings, libraries, and equipment, for greater textbook uniformity, and for better teacher preparation. As objectionable as normal schools later became, they were at the time a godsend, so utterly poor was most teaching. Hundreds of Connecticut schools were eventually improved because of Barnard's efforts.

Unlike Mann, Barnard did not survive the efforts of reform opponents in the legislature. But when they abolished his job he moved on to a similar position in Rhode Island. There he found opposition to public schools to be even stronger. One state legislator declared that his district would never tax itself for schools, not even "at the point of a bayonet," and another stated that one "might as well take a man's ox to plow his neighbor's field as to take his money to educate his neighbor's son." As a result of such attitudes, more than a third of the state's schoolhouses were "absolutely unfit for habitation." Of the fit houses, 200 had no blackboards, maps, globes, clocks, or thermometers, while 270 did not even have windows for ventilation. Worst of all, school rarely met for more than two or three months out of the year.

In time, Barnard saw to it that many of these schools lengthened their terms. The "old delapidated, repulsive, inconvenient houses," he later wrote, gave way to "new, neat, attractive and commodious structures." Indeed, Rhode Island soon came to have one of the highest ratios of acceptable school buildings in the nation. Barnard also helped obtain tax support for schools, and distributed thousands of pamphlets on the subject of school libraries, recommending that they shelve a minimum of 500 volumes per school. He not only argued for teacher training and special teacher institutes, but also for the support of model traveling schools for backcountry people unfamiliar with even the idea of schooling. Barnard's method of publicizing his cause was bolder—and perhaps more impressive to that generation—than was Mann's. For several years, he sponsored the eccentric W. S. Baker's traveling "circus," which went about through the New England backcountry in a covered wagon "selling" education much the same as other traveling shows sold snake oil. Baker would pull into a small settlement with a dozen of his best students, set up blackboards, ring a bell, and hold a session of school. Large crowds gathered and students "showed off," drawing maps, figuring coordinates, computing sums, spelling, and otherwise delighting the appreciative rustics. This kind of showmanship effectively convinced local skeptics of the value of education, and made the idea of tax supported schools much more palatable to a segment of the population that had opposed public schools the most. Barnard himself conducted more than 1,100 meetings and delivered more than 1,500 speeches throughout the state, prompting one observer to estimate that a meeting to promote public schools had been held within three miles of every home during Barnard's stay there. These efforts evidently impressed his former colleagues in Connecticut as well. After seven years in Rhode Island, he resumed his work there, once again as secretary of the State Board of Education.[7]

Barnard, unlike Mann, was essentially a scholar. He is especially remembered for his editorship of the massive, 31-volume *American Journal of Education*. It was one of the most ambitious literary ventures of the 19th Century, and may be the most permanently significant educational journal ever published in the United States. The issues appeared quarterly between 1855 and 1881, by which time they totaled almost 24,000 pages and 12 million words. Now a standard work in college libraries, the *Journal* set occupies more than six feet of shelving. In 1878, the *Encyclopaedia Britannica* called Barnard's *Journal* "by far the most valuable work in our language on the history of education," and even two-thirds of a century later the *Cambridge History of American Literature* declared the *Journal* unsurpassed in "magnitude, scope and quality." Through it, the *History* declared, "Barnard exerted widespread influence on the developing educational interests of America." That, indeed, had been Barnard's purpose in founding the *Journal*. Like Mann, he was convinced that education was a burgeoning profession that would require a substantial, sound literature. A scholarly national publication, he believed, could quicken the pace of professionalization, elevate teaching to a respectable calling, and promote public schools in general. It could be a clearing house for the exchange of ideas, and a national forum for the consideration of important educational issues. Such a journal could spread the educational experiences of New England and Europe to all parts of the United States, most particularly to the underdeveloped Southern region. In brief, the *Journal* could be an instrument to build up a new profession.[8]

Barnard was ideally qualified to edit the *Journal*. His scholarly interests and intellectual abilities had won him a Phi Beta Kappa key at Yale. He traveled widely in America and Europe, and he knew most of the leading intellectuals of his day on both sides of the Atlantic. He visited Europe five times where particularly in Germany he found much of value that could be adapted to American schools. His *Journal* published many accounts of European practices, and present day compulsory education, grading practices, teacher training institutions, methodology, and teacher supervision are all ideas lifted directly from German schools via Barnard's *Journal*. In addition to very omnivorous reading in the theories of education, he could draw on the practical knowledge gained while working on two state boards of education. By virtue of an inherited fortune, he was able to take editorial and financial risks. He did not sacrifice quality for reason of expense, even though hundreds of dollars per volume were paid from his own pocket. The quality and quantity of *Journal* publications undoubtedly enhanced Barnard's reputation. He subsequently became not only president of two colleges but the first U.S. commissioner of education.

Barnard's *Journal* embraced "only articles of permanent value and interest." It eventually included the equivalent of more than 100 treatises on every subject in education history, biography, organization, administration, principles and practices. Among the articles widely read even today include "The Boston Latin Grammar School," "New England Academies," "Biographical Sketch of Horace Mann," "Universities of the Middle Ages," "Schools and Education in Ancient Greece," "Princes in France-Their Education and Teachers," and "Aristotle and His Educational Views."

Significantly, the *Journal* was seldom read by teachers. Not only was its moderate price more than most could pay, but they tended to be "unimaginative plodders" rather than scholars or intellectuals. Horace Mann wrote to Barnard that "most of our people are not up to the level at which you aim." Despite such appeals, however, Barnard never compromised editorial standards for the sake of popularity or to increase circulation. This averaged, incidentally, only about 500 copies per issue. Barnard's primary concern was with the *Journal's* impact, not its profitability. Although the *Journal's* readership was small, it was world-wide.

The question of public schools was an integral part of the other movements in that Age of the Common Man. Americans were moving westward in unprecedented numbers. Opened up as it was to settlers from up and down the Atlantic seaboard, and to tens of thousands of immigrants as well, the entire upper Mississippi valley was the scene of one of history's great hegiras. Wherever the settlers went—to a muddy settlement of 175 houses called Chicago, or to the hog-infested, muddy streets of an even smaller village called Cincinnati, they had to consider school reform. Following a land boom in 1837, New England lumbermen left by the hundreds for Minnesota, then little more than a primitive game reservation for another immigrant, entrepreneur John Jacob Astor. Those who followed took with them the idea of free schools. In 1834 in nearby Wisconsin, settlers plotted three small villages on a map of the Milwaukee River. By the time they were incorporated as the town of Milwaukee 12 years later, a campaign for free schools had already been waged and won. When the state was admitted to the Union in 1848, its new constitution provided for free education for everyone between ages 4 and 20. Michigan also drew settlers from New York and New England who established schools on the New England model. When Michigan was admitted to the Union, there were both constitutional and statutory provisions for education.

The movement veritably exploded thereafter. Missouri established a public school system in 1839, and the Territory of Oregon began operating free schools in 1850. Free public schools were established in Indiana in 1852. In 1855, the First Territorial Legislature of Nebraska adopted its free school law, as did the state of Illinois the same year. Iowa provided free schools for its inhabitants in 1858. Some territories did not wait for statehood: the legislature of Kansas acted in 1859, and that of Dakota provided free schools in 1862.

Everywhere, though, conservative opposition to free schools persisted, just as it did in the other social and political reforms of the period. Many people had not yet shaken off the idea that public schools, like public housing today, were for paupers. They believed that education was something of a frill, a luxury to be purchased according to one's ability and willingness to pay. Others believed that the masses, the great unwashed, were morally and even intellectually unfit for education; and that in any case they had no real need of it. Anticipating the elitist rationale of our own time, some condemned them as "forced schools." Contestants in the free school debate divided along class and ideological lines. Opponents saw no reason why the "thrifty" should have to buy schooling for the "shiftless," and many stated frankly and publicly that free schools rewarded the poor who likely were poor because they deserved to be so. One Watertown, New York, opponent of free schools said that he would "fill the belly" or "cover the back" of a pauper, but he would never send him to school. In the sense that health today is considered a private and not a public matter, education was then considered a personal matter—to be bought and paid for according to one's station and financial position.

As could be expected in that age of newborn evangelical religions, public schools were denounced by many preachers defending the social *status quo*. The pious Mann was accused of atheism, and many predicted that his schools would produce a generation of "irreligious and infidel youth." In a sermon called "The Ark of God on a New Cart," the Reverend Matthew Hale Smith blamed school reformers for an increase in juvenile crime in Boston. No wonder, said others: children educated beyond their stations in life were rootless beings belonging to no class. The more gullible rural parishoners agreed: Children, observed one, "should pass their days in the cotton patch, or at the plow, or in the cornfield instead of being mewed up in a schoolhouse." Bigots, intolerants, aristocrats and monopolists, seemed to be working in tandem to discredit the movement. Few had the larger vision of one conservative leader, Daniel Webster, who regarded education as "a wise and liberal system of police, by which property and life and the peace of society are secured." Indeed, the cause of economic stability and social peace had been an important factor in the founding of public schools on the western frontier. If schools were not used as "a means of teaching frontier folk sound economic doctrines," one observer warned his fellow citizens, pocketbooks would be emptied by a repudiation of credit. Noting developments in Europe instead of at home, a fearful pundit predicted that the reformers would bankrupt and "Prussianize" the United States, open it up to "infidel socialism," and drive it as far as Fourierism (communism).

Opposition arose from less lofty sources than ideology. Immigrants, for example, feared that their children would forget their native traditions and customs when placed in multi-ethnic American schools. Nativists were obsessed with that same vision, arguing that because immigrants were the poor segment of any community, the taxes of established citizens would be grieviously wasted to educate the uninvited hordes, newcomers who multiplied "like rabbits in a burrow," who would undermine society. One prominent Hoosier even directed that his tombstone should read: "Here lies an enemy of free schools." Disingenuous opponents asserted that free schools would do the poor an actual disservice. Repeating the adage that nothing was valued highly if it was obtained for nothing, such schools would undermine respect for those who had obtained fortune and status through private education. (To be sure, men of fortune and status were among the ranks of the reformers as well).[10]

Perhaps the most serious opposition came from the conservative leaders of the South who considered the movement for educational reform as another example of the forces that were threatening that region's very existence. One of the ominous signs of the sectional controversy that worsened in the 1850's was the removal by prominent families of their sons and daughters from the schools of the Northeast. In the latter area, those who viewed all reforms as part of a great effort to better the nation itself generally supported the cause of Union. After a half million men upheld that cause on the battlefieds of the Civil War, several of those same reformers recognized a great opportunity for education in the devastated South. In the tradition of Mann and Barnard they would strive as mightily, but they would have far leaner success.

Four

[1] Quoted in Jonathan Messerli, *Horace Mann* (New York: Alfred A. Knopf, 1972), pp. 59-62. Chapter 4 follows Messerli throughout.

[2] A view of the social and educational conditions prevailing at the outset is in Nye, *Cultural Life*, pp. 124-170. For a description of district schools, see Warren Burton, *The District School As It Was By One Who Went To It*, ed. Clifton Johnson (Boston: Lee & Shepard, 1897; reprint ed., New York: Arno Press, 1969).

[3] On Mann's schooling, Messerli, *Horace Mann*, pp. 59-62. See also pp. 164, 230, 245, 259, 339. See also Samuel Fisher, *Litchfield Law School, 1774-1833, Biographical*

Catalogue for Students (New Haven: Yale University Press, 1933), pp. 27-31.

⁴ Messerli, *Horace Mann*, pp. 242-50. A discussion of Mann's services to reform movements other than educational is in Merle Curti, *The Social Ideas of American Educators* (New York: Charles Scribner's Sons, 1935; reprint ed. Totowa, New Jersey: Littlefield, Adams & Co., 1974), pp. 101-38.

⁵ Mann's initial efforts are described in Messerli, *Horace Mann*, 279-304. See also William A. Mowry, *Recollections of a New England Educator, 1838-1908* (New York: n.p., 1908) for Mann's personality traits. For details concerning the rise of the normal school, which was slow because of the hostility of teachers themselves to it, see Adolph E. Meyer, *An Educational History of the American People* (New York: McGraw-Hill, 1957), pp. 206-7. To teachers, the normal school was a "piffle," and a slur on their competence; and to academicians, it was beneath contempt, an object of open derision. This is because students and their teachers were generally of low ability and of the laboring or working class. In the beginning, normal schools were no more sophisticated than modern day elementary schools. Their diplomas were almost never acceptable for college entrance.

⁶ Messerli, *Horace Mann*, p. 304. See also Mary Mann's "Sr. D. F. Sarimento," *American Journal of Education* 16 (1866): 593-98. See also 1 (1856), p. 729.

⁷ Robert B. Downs, *Henry Barnard*, (Boston: G. K. Hall and Co., 1977), pp. 17-19; 29-32. See also Curti, *Social Ideas*, pp. 156-57.

⁸ Downs, *Henry Barnard*, pp. 30-31. See also *Encyclopaedia Britannica*, 9th ed., s.v. "Education." See also, William P. Trent, et. al., *The Cambridge History of American Literature* (New York: n.p., 1943), p. 404.

⁹ Richard E. Thursfield, *Henry Barnard's American Journal of Education* (Baltimore: Johns Hopkins University Press, 1945), p. 75. Examples of journal coverage are p. 54.

¹⁰ See Daniel Webster's *Works* (Boston: Little Brown & Co., 1854) I, pp. 41-42. See also Curti, *Social Ideas*,

p. 68, and Frank Tracey Carlton, *Economic Influences Upon Educational Progress in the United States, 1820-1850* (Madison: University of Wisconsin Press, 1908), pp. 45-71. For reactionary opposition to public schools, see Zach. Montgommery, *The School Question From A Parental and Non-Sectarian Standpoint* (Washington: Gibson, 1886), and Matthew Hale Smith, *The Bible, The Rod, and Religion in Common Schools* (Boston: Redding & Co., 1847), pp. 10-11. See also Edgar W. Knight, *Education in the United States* (Boston: Ginn and Company, 1929), p. 250; Ellwood P. Cubberley, *Public Education in the United States* (Boston: Houghton Mifflin Co., 1919), pp. 164-66; and Charles L. Coon, *The Beginnings of Public Education in North Carolina* (Raleigh: Edwards & Broughton, 1908), p. 432.

FIVE
Moving A Mountain - I

"We shall plant the New England institution of common schools liberally ... in the great valley of the Mississippi."

George Peabody, 1866

In the span of a single lifetime, that of the Civil War generation, an agrarian republic became an industrial world power. A high rate of natural increase, together with mass immigration, moved population totals from 30 million in 1860, to more than 100 million in 1920. While everyman worshipped material success, thousands of entrepreneurs exploited cheap labor, abundant resources, and laissez-faire governments to amass great fortunes. Railroads created national and international markets, and cattle and mining kingdoms flourished. Even the devastated South arose to new life. Steel, iron, lumber and tobacco industries flourished and planters—only recently dispossessed of their slaves—more than doubled their pre-war production of cotton. These changes affected the quantities and qualities of American education, generally along demographic lines. In the increasing urban parts of the nation, school terms doubled and tripled in length. Thousands of small school districts were consolidated into larger administrative units and schoolbuildings were enlarged and given improved equipment. Normal school graduates, many of them now women, replaced the host of itinerant and often ignorant school masters. These new teachers relied on kindness and reasonableness to conduct their classes instead of the birch switch and the ruler. As the standards of schooling improved, the stigma associating poverty and public education diminished, particularly in the mid-Atlantic states. When laws prohibiting minors in factories were passed late in the period, school attendance began to double and triple. Notably, also, there was a sharp decline in the percentage of youth who did not attend school at all.

In the new states of the Plains and Mountain West, the mythical illiterate—typified by Huckleberry Finn and his father—had long held sway. A governor of the old Northwest Territory testified that Indiana contained the "most ignorant people in the world." "Not a fiftieth man," he wrote in 1790, could read or write.[2] Wilderness illiteracy extended from Tennessee—whose sons Andrew Johnson and Davy Crockett could not read or write until they were grown—all the way to the Pacific Ocean.[3] Ignorance was not an accident, however, nor charmingly romantic in consequence. The tragic but true pun that education was studiously avoided particularly applied to the population of the South. There were no state systems of public education in that region before the Civil War, and no common schools, except for a very few in the largest cities. Many of the thousands of children who were not excluded from schools by expensive rate bills (*pro rata* fees paid by parents according to the number of children they had in school), were shut out by the ridicule heaped upon those who attended free of charge. To send a child to school without paying his way was to advertise desperate financial straits. Few parents were willing to make that admission, even though most families lived a marginal existance. With the exception of some 9,000 scattered planter families who owned most of the South's 4 million slaves, a large majority of the remaining 6 million people in the South were "poor whites." These were divided about equally into the yeoman or petty farmer and the so-called "white trash" classes. Few of this latter class could even sign their names.

These two populations and the slaves were in every sense class brothers: their diets (pork belly, turnip greens, black-eyed peas, cornbread and sweet potatoes), and their shabby cabins, often with earthen floors, were strikingly similar; both dressed in homespuns and went barefoot 10 months of the year. Yet they were at opposite social poles; they were divided by a mutual and very strong enmity that was encouraged and perpetuated by the absence of free schools. That condition in part reflected the assumption by the ruling minority that an educated people might unite themselves, particularly since their interests were the same—and that they might then reject the institution of slavery on which the region's entire economy and society were based. The true motives which underlay opposition to free schools were, however, obscured by the assertion that schools would actually penalize the poor. In a flight of imagery, John Randolph of Roanoke directed the attention of the Virginia Constitutional Convention of 1829 to

> that ragged fellow staggering from the whiskey shop, and see that slattern who has gone to reclaim him; where are their children? Running about ragged, idle, ignorant, fit candidates for the penitentiary. Why is all this so? Ask the man and he will tell you, 'Oh, the government has undertaken to educate our children for us. It has given us a premium for idleness, and I now spend in liquor what I should otherwise be obliged to save for their schooling.'[4]

Poor whites themselves shared this reasoning. Others objected to free schools on the ground that they infringed upon property rights and interfered with the prerogative of parents to educate their children as they saw fit.

While these whites were barred from education by custom, the blacks were prohibited from attending schools by law. Four million blacks were denied even the rudiments of learning, not as a punishment, but as a positive benefit to them. Reading would only further their discontent, their owners reasoned. What these "flesh-eating, blood-drinking, gluttonous, lazy and debased" Africans needed to know first, the *Debow's Review* declared in 1855, was how to "plow, reap, forge, build, paint, weave and print."[5] Civilized to that extent, they might *then* be ready for book learning. But for the present, the *Review* echoed the leaders of the South, the institution of slavery itself was the best kind of education for blacks. At that early stage of their development, they needed skills far more than they needed book learning.

During the Civil War, loyalists to the cause of reunion included many men particularly interested in establishing a modern educational system in the South as soon as the war should end. They meant to bring education to Southerners of "all classes, grades, and complexions." Their plans reflected not only humanitarian concerns, but also the belief that the diffusion of schooling throughout the masses of the South would cement the reunion bought by the force of guns. Just a few weeks after that war came to an end, Samuel Green, the president of the National Teachers Association (forerunner of the National Education Association), focused on that task in his keynote address at the organization's sixth annual meeting in Harrisburg, Pennsylvania. "Look at our country as it was before the war," Green began. In the free states, "the public school system prevailed," and it provided a good education for children "of the poor and rich alike." All social classes, "sat together in the same school, were competitors for the same honors, were taught to value personal worth and intrinsic merit . . . rather than the accidents of birth." But what about those states where slavery prevailed? Millions of children of both races were literally "shut out" from an education. "From the necessities of the case," Green continued, "the two sections of the country parted from each other," and they developed "different tastes, different views of life, and different judgments as to the true functions of government." The underlying cause of the late war, he emphasized, was the "fact of a universal education in the North, and a very limited education in the South." No two sections of the country, he said, "can dwell together in peace and harmony where the advantages of education are so widely dissimilar." Now that the war was over, Green concluded, the South must be educated. Only free schools could unify the country and prevent another Civil War. The "national school master," he said, must now go into 'the old slave states" and bring learning to all "without regard to rank, age, or color."[6]

In a similar call for Northern teachers to go into the South, J. P. Wickersham, a Pennsylvania school master, told

68

the convention that the war's conclusion had left "a vast work to be accomplished." There were now more than 4 million blacks scattered over 900,000 square miles of territory, he said, and these people must quickly be lifted "from darkness to light." Clearly, such a herculean task would require "an army of teachers." Wickersham believed that since "the line of free schools (had) marked the line of loyalty to the government" during the "late rebellion," that line must now be pushed all the way "to the Gulf." "The teacher and his spelling book," he said, "must follow the soldier and his musket into the South."[7]

That is precisely what happened. Under the auspices of benevolent, philanthropic and religious associations, hundreds of northern teachers moved South, even before the war's end, and established schools in areas occupied by federal armies. Thousands followed immediately after the war, and by 1869, there were almost 10,000 teachers in schools in every part of the South. Many of these teachers were compassionate, high-minded and idealistic youth who had come to the South to extend liberalism, republicanism, and democracy. They saw their work as being fateful and lasting, even of cosmic proportions. Others came to spread the Gospel, or just for the high adventure of the trip. Some wrote in their letters of application that they were seeking "a warmer climate for reasons of health," prompting the American Missionary Association to advise applicants: "This is not a hygienic association to help invalids try a change of air or travel at others' expense." Whatever their reasons for coming, they set up makeshift schools wherever shelter could be found—in barns, basements, churches, courthouses, military barracks, even in plantation hen houses and open-air pavilions—and they made do with the crudest furniture, which was often limited to shell boxes and ammunition cases for desks and seats. Despite these inconveniences, and even the fact that white children refused to attend the schools because they were integrated, they overflowed with students of all ages. Understandably, these students had a simple, almost childlike faith in the power of schools, and perhaps even an exaggerated sense of their ultimate worth. Some were sure that knowledge had been the source of their former masters' power, and that schooling assured a life of comfort and ease. Stories reached every section of the country that the freedmen had an "unbounded enthusiasm" and a "universal desire" for learning. Their schools, one observer wrote, had "all the glamor of the new and the strange," and their books particularly had that special "attraction which is characteristic of all forbidden fruit."[8]

With the end of Reconstruction governments in the former Confederate states, Yankee teachers began to leave the South. Despite their good intentions, they had never been cordially received, but had instead been thought of as "carpetbaggers," outsiders, do-gooders, and misguided zealots who represented a philosophy completely alien to Southern customs and traditions. Poor whites were especially jealous of the solicitude of blacks and their attempts to treat blacks as equals. As traditional social attitudes returned, the prospect of thousands of blacks who could read and write caused Southerners to view Yankee teachers with alarm. At first they had only refused to speak to them or to permit them into their churches, or to sell to them, even for cash. But increasingly teachers became objects of ridicule and laughter, taunts, sneers, derision and curses. One New York paper reported that not one head of a household in a thousand had the "moral courage to brook the odium which would be visited upon him" should he "take in" a Northern teacher as a boarder. Some teachers were even burned out, beaten and shot. As the Hernando (Mississippi) *People's Press* explained, blacks educated by "Cape Cod schoolmarms swarming into the South" would be eminently more dangerous to the South than the Yankees themselves.[9]

While the northerners' zeal flagged under such conditions, many southerners expressed interest in taking over the job of teaching blacks. Thousands who just five years earlier had pronounced blacks mentally incapable of book learning, now joined in a general clamor aimed at ridding the South of New England schoolmarms, and replacing them with teachers from the South. An 1867 issue of the Montgomery (Alabama) *Advertiser* stated that there would be "no discredit in it" at all if many of the Southern men who had been "disabled for active work" by the war, were now to find "renumerative labor in teaching colored children." The editor believed that it would even be a positive benefit for the "young men and women in the South to teach their fomer slaves." After all, the books used by Yankee teachers were "embellished with all sorts of false stories," and this would continue to "be the case as long as strangers" came in to teach. "Let the southern people themselves" do this job. Other newspapers took up the challenge. The Petersburg (Virginia) *Index*, for example, admonished that "either we of the South" must teach blacks, or the work would be done by strangers and enemies who would "alienate them from us and use them as a power to perpetuate our political degredation."[10]

Although their stay in the South was of short duration, the influence of these "Cape Cod" teachers can hardly be overestimated. Not only did they teach the first generation of free blacks to read and write—and many of these became teachers themselves and further "diffused the light"—but by doing so, poor whites were made more receptive to the idea of free schools, lest their own children should fall behind the detested blacks in their learning.

At the same time schoolteachers went into the field to reclaim southern children, several individuals brought about significant improvements by their own efforts. The two most notable of these were George Peabody, an expatriate millionaire philanthropist, and his opposite number, Booker T. Washington, a former slave, born on a pile of rags on a plantation cabin's dirt floor.

Peabody had ben a precocious New England youth who, lacking family connections and formal education, left home in 1806 at age 11 to serve a four-year apprenticeship in a retail store. There he acquired enough business skill to become at age 16 the sole support of his family, and at age 23, a prosperous, well-heeled merchant in Washington, D. C. By middle age, Peabody was an international investment banker, a world-recognized merchant prince affiliated with Elisha Riggs, founder of the Washington bank that still bears his name, and with Junius Morgan, father of J.

Pierpont Morgan, founder of another well-known family of American bankers.

Peabody was cordial, yet taciturn, unmarried, but the father of at least one child. Despite an innate revulsion to wasting time, he nonetheless walked to business appointments to save cab fares, and he practiced other petty, unnecessary economies to the secret amusement of all who knew him. He was usually—but not always— honest. The machinations on which his immense fortune was established—the sale of bonds to finance construction of the B. and O. Railroad and the Chesapeake & Ohio Canal—have never been fully unraveled. (Gustavus Myers' *History of Great American Fortunes* asserts that Peabody's actions in both cases were objectionable and dishonest). Peabody gave away millions to libraries, museums and universities, and his philanthropies inspired the establishment of the John F. Slater and the Anna T. Jeanes funds, which later merged with his Fund for Southern Education to become the Southern Education Foundation. Peabody was also influential in the founding of Tulane and Johns Hopkins universities and the Johns Hopkins Medical School. He was much more directly responsible for the establishment of George Peabody for Teachers in Nashville, Tennessee.[11]

Even though Peabody lived permanently in London, and ran his vast business empire from there, he did not give up his American citizenship, nor did he ever waver during the war in his private sympathy for the Union. But he chose after the war to leave much of his private fortune to "encourage the intellectual, moral and industrial education of the destitute children of the Southern states," those who had been hardest hit by the war. Accordingly, he set up the Peabody Fund for Southern Education. Peabody insisted that the fund be administered with a broad view. There was no place on his Board of Trustees for those still ridden with sectional prejudices, but beyond that Peabody insisted only that the trustees be eminent in their chosen fields, and that they come from widely different backgrounds. General Ulysses S. Grant was a charter member of the board, as was South Carolina planter William Aiken, whose cotton and rice plantation, *Jehossee*, had been destroyed during the war. Other trustees at various times inlcuded Rutherford B. Hayes, Hamilton Fish, Grover Cleveland and J. Pierpont Morgan.

The fund's first general agent was Barnas Sears, a strikingly handsome former president of Brown University. Sears had replaced Horace Mann as secretary to the Massachusetts State Board of Education when Mann resigned to run for Congress.[12] He knew intimately the logistics of school reform, and he had his own ideas as to how Mann's New England movement could be transplanted to the South. It was for these reasons that the Peabody board named him as its first general agent. Sears directed the fund brilliantly, giving it its initial direction. It was he who determined that Peabody's money would be more than mere charity to be handed out to the poor. And neither would the Peabody Fund be just another of the many agencies working in tandem (and ineffectually) with the religious and philanthropic groups that heretofore had always looked after the education of Southern children. Sears wished to strike out on a new path, and fundamentally change for the better the whole scheme, such as it was, of Southern education. His idea was that the fund should offer incentives to communities all over the South to set up their own schools. He would not pay for the schools himself, nor would he even lend all the money necessary to establish the schools. But he would lend 25% of a project's cost on condition that local initiative finance the remaining costs. As Sears conceived it, he should work directly with state and local authorities, not with private groups. And the biggest part of his work would be to stimulate interest in public schools in the South, just as Mann and Barnard had done in New England.

Shortly after his appointment, Sears made an inspection tour of school conditions all over the South. He spoke to state legislatures, colleges and teachers' associations, and he met privately with leading citizens who knew first hand the educational problems of the South. In all of this he determined that the major needs of Southern education were for state departments of education, state teacher groups and professional associations, good educational journals, and a goodly supply of teachers who, he felt, should

73

be trained in state normal schools rather than in the teacher training departments of academies and colleges.

Sears depended on Peabody money to achieve all of these goals. He kept records, made disbursements, figured the actual needs of hundreds of communities which wanted to set up their own schools, and he often supervised their establishment as well. He spoke out at every opportunity for state established, supported and controlled free and universal education for Southern children. Significantly, Sears accomplished this under the most adverse conditions. Most Southerners resented "Cape Cod" schoolmen like himself; many office holders were corrupt and incompetent; property values had plummeted; school funds were squandered in kickback schemes; state treasuries were empty; and state bonds were recklessly sold at huge discounts to finance unwise appropriations. Moreover, Sears did his work in a region where people with little experience in financing and operating schools, and with even less taste for either, adhered to the ultimate fear—that state supported education would bring mixed (integrated) schools, possible miscegenation, and worst of all, collapse of the only way of life they knew. Sears' policy of lending a percentage of a school's original cost substantially increased the true value of Peabody's original benefaction and lent stability and permanence to school systems which continued to operate long after Peabody funds were withdrawn. Most of the schools and projects which Sears financed became self-supporting in a short period of time.[13]

Perhaps the ugliest chapter in the fund's history involved the issue of school integration, a hotly debated subject in the 1870's. Sears was adamantly opposed to "mixed" schools, and gave as his reasons his belief that integration would reverse the growing acceptance of universal education in the South, undo the good the fund had already done, and plunge the South into renewed bitter conflict. Just how much his opposition owed to class or racial antipathies, or to his own conservatism or to that of the trustees, or even to his dependence upon the good will of Southerners for his reputation and job effectiveness, it is impossible to say. In any case, his motives cannot be entirely judged in light of prevailing social views. Perhaps he was just willing to go slow in order to neutralize hostility, and thus make at least a *beginning* in the movement to bring free schools to the South. Sears was critical of, and he lobbied against a Louisiana experiment with integrated schools, and he denounced those like Senator Charles Sumner "and his trained negroes" who favored them. He himself adamantly stipulated that only segregated schools were eligible for Peabody aid, and that white schools, being costlier to operate, were entitled to one-third more aid money than black schools. Such actions raise a question as to whether his misgivings with integration were real or merely a subterfuge concocted to freeze history for a few more decades.[14]

It should be noted that in all of these things relating to the integration controversy, Sears was sustained by the fund's Board of Trustees who declared that "compulsory legislation by Congress in favor of mixed schools would be most pernicious to the interests of education . . . and the colored population would suffer the greater share of this disastrous influence."[15]

Sears explained his lobbying efforts against the school integration clause of the Civil Rights Act of 1875 in a letter to the trustee chairman on January 8, 1874. He reported that he had gone to Washington to seek the "omission or modification" of that clause in Massachusetts Representative Ben Butler's Civil Rights Bill "which relates to schools." While there, he spoke not only with Butler but with Representative George Hoar, also of Massachusetts, and with others, both in the House and Senate, protesting the integration clause. Congress should "omit the school integration clause altogether," he told them, or at least "require only equal privileges of education without mixing the two races in the schools." "I think I convinced them all," Sears wrote, "that the Bill would overthrow the State systems of free schools, and leave both the blacks and poor whites . . . destitute of schools altogether" since if the bill were passed intact "private schools would be substituted for public." Then, Sears called on "leading Senators . . . who will see that the objectionable clause is left out or changed, or that the Bill is defeated in the Senate." Lastly, he visited the White House and reported that President Grant not only viewed "the subject as we do," but "told General Butler . . . that it was unwise to attempt to force mixed schools upon the South."

Although the deletion of the bill's integration clause owed more to political considerations than to the concerns of educators like Sears, there is little doubt that Representative Butler was dissuaded from pressing the school proviso by his old field commander, now President Grant, who was himself a charter member of the Peabody Fund Board of Trustees. The Peabody board included at various times two other presidents of the United States, two chief justices of the Supreme Court, admirals, generals, bishops, senators, representatives, ambassadors, mayors, governors, academicians, and financiers. Its political influence was thus formidable. The Civil Rights Bill was passed without the integration clause, and many believed that Sears had saved the burgeoning public school system in the South from disaster. "Actually," wrote one scholar of the Reconstruction period, "he merely helped delay its coming to terms with social reality, a postponement for which succeeding generations would have to pay the price." Failure to federally enforce school integration in the 1870's "made acceptance of this social and legal necessity a far more difficult task 90 years later."[16]

After Sears' death in 1880, Jabez Lamar Monroe Curry succeeded him as general agent for the Peabody Fund. A graduate of Harvard Law School, Curry was at different times a representative in both the United States and Confederate congresses, a college president, and a minister to Spain. His statue is exhibited in Statuary Hall in the United States Capitol. Curry's appointment was a turning point in the fund's history. When he took office, state systems of public education had already been established throughout the South, and public opinion had shifted to the point where the continued growth of the systems seemed assured. It remained then for Curry to direct the fund's efforts toward the improvement of teaching, and with this goal in mind, he encouraged the establishment of normal schools throughout the South on the model of the Peabody School at Nashville, Tennessee. The promotion of these schools had been the fund's goal from the beginning, Curry explained, but until the southern states "had committed themselves thoroughly to . . . public free schools, this was held in . . . abeyance." In assessing Peabody's impact on American education, Curry wrote that when the fund was established in 1867, "not a single southern state provided a public school system for its children." Moreover, except for in a few cities, there were no public schools at all in the South. "Illiteracy," he wrote, was "appalling," and was "by no means confined to freedmen," but included a large part of the white population as well. The fund had "made a vigorous and persistent effort to induce the states to include free and universal education among their permanent obligations; and the effort was rewarded with early success." Every one of the southern states now had a system of public schools.

The work of northern educators also inspired the best initiatives taken by former slaves. Booker T. Washington, born in Hales Ford, Virginia, in 1856, was 16 years old when he enrolled in Hampton Institute. That school had been founded just four years earlier by the charismatic Samuel C. Armstrong, who had been a general in the U.S. Army at the precocious age of 26.[17] Born on the island of Maui, in the Hawaiians, his New England parents had been among the first missionaries sent out to Hawaii by the American Board of Missions. Armstrong's school reflected his military background in that students were inspected daily in their barracks for personal cleanliness. The idea was to "clean up" the manners, morals and hygienic habits of these former slaves so as to make them more pleasing to white sensibilities, and thus smooth the way to their eventual integration into white society. Armstrong's school also reflected his own schooling at Williams College in Massachusetts under the tutelage of Mark Hopkins, whom President James Garfield later immortalized; and the school was a copy in many ways of the thatch-roofed school in Hawaii in which his missionary father had taught the gentle but sinful natives to wear clothes and speak pidgin English. Armstrong's view of blacks, in fact, was as paternalistic as his father's view of the Polynesians. But years later, Booker T. Washington, a graduate of Hampton, wrote that

Armstrong was of that "Christlike body of men and women who went into the Negro schools at the close of the war . . . to assist in uplifting my race." History failed to show, Washington wrote, "a higher, purer, and more unselfish class of men and women than those who found their way into those Negro schools."[18]

Washington had founded his own school at Tuskegee, Alabama, in 1881, and had modeled it after the Hampton school. Like Armstrong, he was determined not to turn out pedants or over-educated dandies who would never survive, he felt, in a world so different from the one they had been born into, and where for the first time in their lives they would be completely on their own. Like Armstrong, Washington wanted to give students something practical, something "more than mere books." He insisted first on "civilizing" his charges, teaching them the barest rudiments—"how to bathe" he wrote, "how to care for their teeth and clothing" and "what to eat, and how to eat it properly." Aside from this he wanted "to give them such a practical knowledge of trade, together with a spirit of industry, thrift and economy, that they would be sure of knowing how to make a living after they had left us."

The curriculum at Tuskegee included building trades, which were learned by actually building the school dormitories and classrooms—brick by home-made brick—from the ground up. Students cleared land, and grew and canned their own food, serving it later in the school cafeteria. They raised cash crops; they learned gardening, fruit growing, dairying, bee culture, and poultry raising. They marketed hogs, cattle, turkeys and eggs, and they made and sold mattresses, wagons and furniture. Their home-made bricks were of the first quality (and some of their original structures still stand). At first, Washington had a difficult time in getting some students to work. They had just been freed from hard labor, they said; they were the talented tenth of black society, and they would work with their heads or not at all. But his message was one of self-reliance, hard work, fitting in and getting along; and when necessary to make a point, he plowed the fields, uprooted stumps, and fed the chickens himself—alongside his students—thus dignifying honest labor of any sort in their eyes. They could always learn Latin and Greek, he told them. But for the present they needed to learn how to survive. Within a few years the 2,300 acre plantation Washington bought—mostly on a promise to pay—was completely paid off, and Tuskegee was sending hundreds of graduates each year, the first cadre of black teachers ever, into the cane-breaks and river bottoms of the South to teach all of these skills to other blacks, so recently and so abruptly thrown on their own resources.

Although Hampton and Tuskegee were critical to the advancement of blacks, the long-term accomplishments of Booker T. Washington are not generally agreed upon. Washington was, of course, a controversial figure during his lifetime. Thereafter, his detractors and defenders divided along ideological lines. In the former group, W. E. B. Du Bois believed that the "schoolbook hero" myth that surrounded Washington was contrived by reactionary elements in society who agreed with his views that schools should be segregated, that militancy and labor agitation were harmful to the country, and that less than full citizenship should be accepted by blacks on a temporary basis. Others condemned him as an accommodationist and a class collaborator. They despised his humility, his self-effacement and his eagerness to "keep his place."[19] They judged him an embarrassment to progressive elements in both races, an autocrat wielding philanthropic money, or a benevolent despot in charge of a political force so powerful that it came to be called the "Tuskegee Machine."

His defenders on the other hand see Washington as a black Moses whose works literally lifted an entire people "up from slavery" and provided a foundation for their future advancement. His pragmatic bargains with the South, they say, neutralized hostility and held out the only hope for even beginning what would become a long and often sorrowful struggle for equality. Washington challenged blacks to help themselves: he told them that bondage was no longer an excuse for ignorance, and he established in full view and in hostile territory (where the American flag wasn't flown until World War I), a command post from which the social advance of blacks could be planned and directed. Had he militantly thrown down the gauntlet (as many urged), and demanded a greater and more immediate leap foreward, defenders say, the chances of success would almost certainly have been greatly diminished.

As thousands of Hampton and Tuskegee graduates helped set up their own primitive black schools all over the rural South, and as tens of thousands of poor whites began attending the schools made possible for them by men like George Peabody and Barnas Sears, the long fight for free public schools in the United States drew to a close. Now at least a start had been made in educating all levels of society in all sections of the country.

Five

[1] Quoted in Jabez Monroe Curry, *A Brief Sketch of George Peabody and a History of the Peabody Education Fund Through Thirty Years* (Cambridge: University Press, 1898; reprint ed., New York: Negro University Press, 1969) p. 3.

[2] Quoted in Edgar W. Knight, *Education in the United States* (Boston: Ginn and Company, 1929) p. 228.

[3] But much was done to combat wilderness and frontier illiteracy. William Holmes McGuffey, for example, taught on the Ohio frontier at age 14. During his first four-month winter session he taught 48 students for 11 hours a day, six days a week. Later, McGuffey compiled his famous eclectic reader. See John H. Westerhoff, *McGuffey and His Readers* (Nashville: Abingdon Press, 1978) pp. 32-33.

[4] Randolph quoted in the *Richmond Enquirer*, November 24, 1829, as cited by Frederick M. Binder, *The Age of the Common School, 1830-1865* (New York: John Wiley and Sons, 1974) pp. 136-37. President Andrew Johnson had these people in mind when he stated that the Civil War emancipated more whites than blacks. See also A. O. Craven, "Poor Whites and Negroes in the Antebellum South," *Journal of Negro History* 15 (1939): 14-26. See also Adolph E. Meyer, *An Educational History of the American People* (New York: McGraw-Hill Book Company, 1957) p. 209.

[5] *Debow's Review*, Volume 18 (1855): 666.

⁶ Samuel Green, "The Educational Duties of the Hour," *American Journal of Education* 16 (1866): 229-43.

⁷ J. P. Wickersham, "Education As an Element In Reconstruction," *American Journal of Education* 16 (1866): 283-97.

⁸ Henry Lee Swint, *The Northern Teacher in the South 1862-1870* (Nashville: Vanderbilt University Press, 1941) pp. 35-97, 138. Most missionary schools forbade racial segregation on the ground that it was "inherently wrong," and that once begun, segregated schools would not be easily abandoned. See C. G. Woodson, *The Education of the Negro Prior to 1861* (Washington, D.C.: Associated Publishers, 1919; reprint ed., New York: Arno Press and the New York Times, 1968). Some of the teachers' interesting diaries and other works have been published. See for example, Charles Stearns, *The Black Man of the South and the Rebels* (New York: American News Company, 1872; reprint ed., New York: Negro Universities Press, 1969).

⁹ For accounts of the work of these teachers, and of how they were despised, whipped, stoned, and burned out, see Julius H. Parmelee, "Freedmen's Aid Societies, 1861-1871," *Negro Education*, Bureau of Education, Bulletins No. 38-39, v. I, Washington, D.C., 1916, pp. 244 ff. See also Walter L. Fleming, *Documentary History of Reconstruction* (Cleveland: n.p., 1907) v. II, pp. 165 ff. As Yankee teachers pulled up stakes in Petersburg, Virginia, the *Richmond Times* reported that townspeople were bearing up magnificently under the strain. Their loss, the *Times* sarcastically reported, was being accepted with "philosophic if not with Christian resignation." The *Times* then wondered if Africa might not be a suitable new mission field. There the teachers might become "gastronomic if not educational successes!" See William Preston Vaughn, *Schools For All* (Lexington: University of Kentucky Press, 1974), p. 33.

¹⁰ Quotes are in Alrutheus A. Taylor, *The Negro in the Reconstruction of Virginia* (Washington: Association for the Study of Negro Life and History, 1926) p. 151; and Montgomery (Alabama) *Advertiser*, July 24, 1867, cited by W. L. Fleming, *Documentary History of Reconstruction*, 2 vols. (Cleveland: n.p., 1906-07) 2: 181.

¹¹ Some of Peabody's other projects survive his death by more than a century, one being a complex of model dwellings and flats given to the workers of the Spitalfields

district of London who previously had lived in squalid slum conditions. In gratitude for this work, Queen Victoria offered to confer a title, but Peabody declined because he was unwilling to give up his American citizenship. Even though 30 blocks of these buildings were destroyed in bombing raids during World War II, more than 7,000 units were standing at the end of the war. See Franklin Parker, *George Peabody* (Nashville: Vanderbilt University Press, 1971) pp. 124-28. For more on Peabody's illegitimate daughter, see Parker, *Peabody*, pp. 32-33. For the part played by philanthropy in the educational development of the South—gifts of John F. Slater ($1 million), John D. Rockefeller ($130 million), Mrs. Russell Sage ($10 million), and Julius Rosenwald, Sears and Roebuck executive, ($63 million), see Franklin Parker, "George Peabody's Influence on Southern Philanthropy," *Tennessee Historical Quarterly* 20, (1961), 65-74. See also Daniel Gilman, "Five Great Gifts," *Outlook* 86 (1907): 645-57.

[12] Sears and Mann were not friends. In an *intrigue academe* while President of Brown University, Sears had blocked the award of an honorary doctorate to Mann, much to Mann's disgust. See Thursfield, *Barnard's American Journal*, p. 129.

[13] Curry, *Brief Sketch*, pp. 38-39.

[14] For interpretations of Sears' motives, see Earle H. West, "The Peabody Fund and Negro Education, 1867-1880," *History of Education Quarterly* 6 (1966): 13-21. For a revealing account of the attitudes of many Southerners toward schooling for blacks at this time, see "Report of the Joint Committee on Reconstruction," *House Reports*, No. 30, Part 2, 39th Congress, 1st. Session.

[15] Curry, *Brief Sketch*, p. 64.

[16] William Preston Vaughn, "Partners in Segregation: Barnas Sears and the Peabody Fund," *Civil War History* 10 (1964): 274. See also his "Separate and Unequal: The Civil Rights Act of 1875 and Defeat of the School Integration Clause," *Southwestern Social Science Quarterly* 48 (1967): 154. While the Act was silent on the subject of schools, it prohibited segregation in hotels, theaters, and on public carriers. Those provisions were invalidated in 1883 when the Supreme Court declared the act to be unconstitutional.

[17] For another portrait of Armstrong, see Donald

Spivey, *Schooling for the New Slavery: Black Industrial Education, 1868-1915* (Westport, Conn.: Greenwood Press, 1978).

[18] Booker T. Washington, *Up From Slavery* (New York: Doubleday & Co., 1900) pp. 54-62. See also Louis R. Harlan, *Booker T. Washington* (New York: Oxford University Press, 1972) p. 59.

[19] Washington, habitually grinned, "massahed," and yanked off his hat, even to 14 and 15 year old white boys.

SIX
Moving A Mountain - II

"No tea for the feeble, no crepe for the dead . . . "

**Black lawyer Charles Houston,
1936**

The extension of public education to most black Americans fell short of Horace Mann's democratic ideal. The advocates of that program did not—or could not—effectively enlist the powers of government in their crusade as Mann had in his 50 years before. To be sure, the climate of opinion on such matters greatly changed in that interval of time, especially in legislatures and courts. The persistence after the Civil War of the tradition of segregated schools is confirmed by the practice of that policy in New York, Chicago, Philadelphia, San Francisco and many other cities of the North and West as well as the South. Even Boston, the center of human rights reforms, held fast to such institutionalized discrimination. Indeed, that city provided the legal rationale for segregation.

In 1849, the Massachusetts Supreme Court heard a case that was the sensation of the day. Five-year-old Sarah Roberts had been required to attend Boston's Smith Grammar School for black children. Its run-down condition, cramped rooms, defaced walls and shattered equipment were a matter of public record. On her way to that school she walked past five better equipped and better managed white schools. When her father requested her reassignment to the school nearest her home, the board of education denied the request. At this point, Boston attorney Charles Sumner, later to become one of the United States Senate's most

85

powerful figures, entered the case on Roberts' side. When the case reached the state Supreme Court, his arguments were followed in every section of the country. Sumner pointed out that the board of education's minority report had condemned the illegality and the needless expense of operating separate school systems for white and black children. Moreover, segregated schools could never be equal, he declared, and white children were as seriously harmed by them as black children. "Their hearts," Sumner said, "while yet tender with childhood are necessarily hardened" by such "legalized uncharitableness." Sumner cited sections from the state constitution which he believed outlawed every form of discrimination. It was true, he declared, that school children could be classified by age, sex, or intelligence, or by any other measure reasonably related to the legitimate work of education; but they could *not* be classified simply by color or race. To do so, he said, would be to "brand a whole race with the stigma of inferiority." But it was Sumner's contention that all persons stood on an equal footing before the law that drew the court's closest scrutiny. That was "perfectly sound" reasoning, the court wrote, and in fact that same "great principle" animated "the whole spirit of our constitution of free government." But anticipating the debates over Social Darwinism, the judges asserted that such a principle did not confirm

> that men and women are legally clothed with the same civil and political powers, and that children and adults are legally to have the same functions and be subject to the same treatment; but only that the rights of all, as they are settled and regulated by law, are equally entitled to the paternal consideration and protection of the law . . .

Local districts could, therefore, maintain separate schools for white and black children so long as the schools were equally "well fitted."[1] (This phrasing would later give birth to the "separate but equal" principle).

If the *Roberts* decision could stand in the face of the strong reform impulse in Massachusetts during the subsequent decade, it is not surprising that segregation was upheld in Ohio in 1871, California and Indiana in 1874, New York in 1883, and in Missouri in 1890. Moreover, local option favored *de facto* school segregation in Kansas, Wyoming, New Mexico and Arizona. It was required in the former Confederate states and in the nation's capital as well. In 11 other northern and western states, there were no laws on the subject.[2] But the Supreme Court had provided the legal foundation for school segregation in any state in its decision on *Plessy v. Ferguson* (1896). Having cited *Roberts* in earlier judgments, the high court restated that ruling's key phrase, "well-fitted." States could permit or even require separation of races in places where they were "likely to be brought into contact" (i.e., trains and schools) if those facilities provided "separate but equal" accommodations. Justice John Marshall Harlan, the lone dissenter in *Plessy*, vigorously attacked the decision. "Our constitution is color-blind," he wrote, and "neither knows nor tolerates classes among citizens."[3]

Soon after the time of *Plessy*, the nation's climate of opinion was once again transformed by nearly two decades of social and political reform in which philanthropy and militant organizations once again worked in tandem. In 1922, a 21-year-old Harvard student named Charles Garland created a front-page sensation by renouncing the fortune his father had left and turning it over to the American Fund for Public Service, which came to be called the "Garland Fund." The foundation was expressly established to promote social change. The next year, he presented an additional inheritance from his grandfather, making a total gift to the Fund of $1,300,000 (about $6 million in 1980 dollars). After choosing the general secretary of the small and then insignificant National Association for the Advancement of Colored People (NAACP) as the fund's director, Garland dropped completely from public view. Wishing to live simply and "on a Christian basis," he returned to a life that the *New York Times* described as barely "scraping out a living from a tiny Cape Cod farm."[4]

In 1929, the Fund trustees set aside $100,000 as a grant to finance "a large scale widespread dramatic campaign to

87

give the southern Negro his constitutional rights." The trustees urged that part of the money be used to bring taxpayer's suits throughout the South requiring that black and white schools be made truly equal, as the Supreme Court had required. The long-range purpose of these suits was to make dual school systems so expensive to operate that they would eventually be abandoned in favor of integrated schools. It was also hoped that these maneuverings would focus national attention on the unequal apportionment of tax revenues to white and black schools, and that they would serve as examples, and give courage to others to file and press similar actions. Now, for the first time, the 20-year old NAACP had enough money to frame a legal drive to end public school segregation.

The framing of this long-range strategy began the next year, in 1930, when Nathan Margold was retained as NAACP counselor and strategist. Margold, a Harvard Law School instructor, was chosen on the recommendation of his colleague, Felix Frankfurter. Margold began his work by assembling and studying as a piece the entire record of segregation-related state and federal court decisions. This record stretched from *Roberts* in 1849 to *Plessy* 47 years later, and finally to three sustaining U.S. Supreme Court decisions running through 1927. On analyzing these cases together, Margold concluded, very much to his surprise, that never in 75 years of segregation-related litigation had the courts *directly* confronted the issue of segregation *per se*, the intrinsic question of segregation. Instead, it seemed that they had dealt with the issue on the narrowest possible grounds. Moreover, the Supreme Court had never unqualifiedly upheld segregation, but had always stipulated that if facilities were to be segregated, they must also be "equal." It seemed to Margold that the Court had never been eager "to promote school segregation into an honored principle of American law."

In the months that followed, Margold produced a booklength *Report* on the legal strategies by which *Plessy* might eventually be overturned.[5] In it he argued that the original idea of suing widely separated school districts to provide equal facilities was unsound. Forcing one district into compliance with *Plessy* would have no effect on thousands of similar districts unless state laws were challenged in the process. Moreover, such suits would establish no new principles, and would leave "wholly untouched the . . . essence of the existing evils." In the end, Margold warned, such a long, drawn-out struggle would "do no more than . . . eliminate a very minor part" of the discrimination which existed at the time the suits were brought.

A better approach, he believed, would be to strike at the constitutional validity of segregation itself, and to challenge segregation's legality as it was practiced, not its constitutionality in the abstract. This could best be done by showing that educational equality did not exist in the states which segregated their school systems. Some of these states spent five times as much for educating white children as for blacks, and none had laws requiring school districts to divide funds on a 50-50 basis as *Plessy* had seemed to require. Margold thought that such laws could be struck down as unconstitutional. His strategy was to pick and choose very carefully the cases that could most easily be won, and then to build "a string of precedents, one victory leading to and supporting the next."[6]

Margold's *Report* was a social, legal and educational milestone in the history of the United States. Because of it, segregation, which until then had seemed almost inviolable, came to be seen by many thoughtful people as resting on a weak foundation. Although his ideological heirs did not adopt it to the letter as their strategy, they used the *Report* as the cornerstone of the 25-year movement to end segregation. It pointed the way to that fundamental change in how and with whom people would be educated, and how they came to think and live.

Had it not been for the vision and initiatives of Charles Houston, a Washington, D.C., law school dean, Margold's *Report* might well have been overlooked. At age 15, Houston, a grandson of slaves, had been elected valedictorian of his graduating class at Washington, D.C.'s M Street High School, then one of the best black secondary schools in the country. Four years later he won a Phi Beta Kappa key and graduated *cum laude* from Amherst, a private liberal arts college in Massachusetts. After service as an artillery officer during World War I, he decided to practice law with his father, a leading member of the District of Columbia Bar. Thereafter, he enrolled at Harvard Law School and studied under Felix Frankfurter, whose brilliance had already begun to earn him a national reputation in legal and academic circles. For 2 years Houston was editor of the *Harvard Law Review*, an honor reserved for the highest ranking students. He earned his first law degree in 1922, and his doctorate in law the following year. Then he studied abroad at the University of Madrid and earned another doctorate in civil law. When Houston returned to the United States in 1924, he was probably the best educated black lawyer in the country.

On becoming vice-dean of the unaccredited and little known Howard University Law School in 1929, Houston quickly transformed it into a fully accredited and nationally known institution. Under his direction the school became a laboratory for the training of lawyers who would follow through with the legal inititiatives recommended in the Margold *Report*. Indeed, during the early 1930's, Houston's school became the nerve center for the drive, then gaining momentum, to end public school segregation. Houston was the dominant force and the architect of the early legal efforts to end segregation. He constantly reminded his students at Howard to prepare for the coming all-out civil rights struggle, and to fight it through to the end, never stopping even to take account of those struck down in the fray. "No tea for the feeble," Houston would say, "no crepe for the dead."[7]

Houston's best all-around pupil at Howard was Thurgood Marshall, a 21-year-old West Baltimore youth who, with the help of his schoolteacher-mother and dining car steward-father, had already worked his way through Pennsylvania's Lincoln University. Outgoing, extremely intelligent, wily, and ebullient, Marshall had been one of "Black Princeton's" most popular students. While attending classes, he had held several outside jobs, waiting tables in night clubs and carrying guests' luggage in hotels. Marshall was gregarious, a natural mixer known for his caustic wit and mordant sense of humor. His stories, often told in mock dialect, charmed even his most scathing adversaries.

It seemed a natural merger when Houston and Marshall became law partners for the coming civil rights struggle. Their combination of talents—Houston's gift for abstract thinking and Marshall's engaging extroversion—made the two a superior legal team. Together, they masterminded the opening round of maneuverings to abolish public school segregation that began shortly after Marshall's graduation from Howard in 1933.[8]

The first Houston-Marshall case seemed made to order. Twenty-one year old black Donald Murray was a socially prominent Amherst graduate from Baltimore who had applied for admission to the University of Maryland law school in 1934. The school president had informed Murray that "the University does not accept Negro students except at the Princess Anne Academy," a two-year agricultural school on the Eastern Shore. He advised Murray to either apply for an out-of-state scholarship or take advantage of the lower tuition costs and the "exceptional facilities open to you" at Howard University law school, just 40 miles away. Murray decided that neither of these arrangements was satisfactory. In the first place, there were almost 400 other applicants for the 50 or so $200 "out-of-state" scholarships, for which, incidentally, the legislature had yet to make an appropriation. More importantly, Murray wished to practice law in Maryland (not Washington, D.C.). He believed that a curriculum based on Maryland codes and taught by Maryland professors—many of whom were practicing attorneys and judges, and whose connections were useful to graduates in their placement and careers— would be more beneficial to him than a curriculum based on non-Maryland codes and taught by out-of-state professors.

The reasonableness of Murray's request would not be lost on a fair judge, Houston and Marshall believed, especially since Maryland had no law facility for blacks at all, equal or unequal. Moreover, Murray was seeking admission to a graduate-level professional school where opposition would in no way equal what might be expected at the public school level. That this school was located in a "moderate" border state (not too far below the "Smith and Wesson" line, as Marshall joked referring to the gun used by lynching parties) only improved his chances of winning. Finally, Murray's social prominence, good looks, and quick intelligence would favorably impress almost any court, it was thought. When the case came to trial, Houston and Marshall pointed out that neither state laws nor university regulations forbade Murray's admission. Moreover, they argued, applicants of Mexican, Japanese, Indian and Filipino descent were routinely admitted to the school. So why then not blacks? When the university president answered that only "custom" and "state policy" blocked Murray's admission, the judge ordered him admitted promptly. Murray was accepted matter-of-factly by students and professors, and he was never subjected to an indignity of any kind.[9]

The next year, Houston sued the University of Missouri for refusing to admit 25-year-old St. Louis resident Lloyd Lionel Gaines to its all-white law schools. Like Maryland, Missouri had no law facility at all for blacks. But when the university told the court that such a facility could quickly be provided at all-black Lincoln University at Jefferson City, the court ruled against Gaines. Houston appealed to the U.S. Supreme Court, and in a 6-2 decision, Gaines was ordered admitted to the all-white school. Sensing the future erosion of *Plessy*, the two dissenting justices warned that a breakdown of the "settled practice" of segregating schools would "damnify both races." The year was 1938.[10]

Gaines v. Canada was an important victory. While *Murray* was only a state court decision, *Gaines* had come directly from the U.S. Supreme Court, and it required that every state guarantee equal graduate facilities to students of both races. Court-watchers began to wonder if this principle could soon be extended to include equal undergraduate facilities and equal public school facilities, equal school terms, teacher salaries, and equal bus transportation. In time, perhaps the principle could be extended to include equal libraries, parks, swimming pools, public transportation, hospitals, hotels, restaurants and theaters.

During the decade of New Deal reform, measured partial accommodation for black Americans by federal executive orders evidently satisfied advocates of civil rights. It was not until World War II underscored the persistence of segregation that they returned to their quest for legal redress. In 1947, Marshall sued the University of Oklahoma for refusing to admit 21-year-old Ada Sipuel to its all-white law school. Despite her excellent credentials, which included graduation with honors from an Oklahoma Negro college, and despite the case's similarities to *Gaines* of the previous decade, the court upheld the board of regents in rejecting her application for admission. Not only might the board exclude Sipuel, the court ruled, but it need not build a black school she could attend until there were enough black applicants to make one practicable. The decision was upheld on appeal, and Marshall went to the U.S. Supreme Court. Now, for the first time, he attacked the "separate but equal" principle as a contradiction. The words "separate" and "equal," he said, could never be used conjointly. The court ordered the board of regents to either admit Sipuel to the white facility or build a separate facility for her. Failing one of these options, the board was directed to close its all-white school. In compliance, the regents created a black "law school" overnight by roping off a few rooms in the state capitol and reassigning three teachers there as faculty. Seeing this as a failure to act in good faith, more than 1,000 students demonstrated against the board. Marshall then returned to the U.S. Supreme Court and charged the regents with being evasive. He said that the essence of education was found not in mere facilites but in the free exchange of ideas among students, and that roping a few off from others was a denial of equal education. Marshall argued that segregating students by race automatically imputed a badge of inferiority. The Supreme Court disagreed, however, and ruled that the regents had acted in good faith. The makeshift law school would have to do. As a result, *Sipuel* seemed to be a setback.[11]

While *Sipuel* was still being decided, Marshall brought another suit against the University of Oklahoma for refusing to admit 68-year-old George McLaurin to the graduate school of education where he wished to earn a doctoral degree. When he was later admitted on orders of a federal judge, McLaurin was not permitted inside classrooms. Instead, he was required to sit in an empty room next door where he could listen to lectures, although, of course, he could not participate in class discussions. He was also required to sit at a segregated desk in an isolated section of the library, and at a segregated table in an alcove adjoining the college cafeteria. Meals could be taken there, but only at different hours from other students. When the district court ruled that these obviously ridiculous restrictions were not unreasonable, Marshall appealed to the U.S. Supreme Court in the case of *McLaurin v. Oklahoma State Regents for Higher Education* (1950). The restrictions were modified almost overnight enabling McLaurin to attend classes and even venture onto the main floor at the library. He could also take his meals in the cafeteria at regular hours now, but in all classes he must continue to sit at segregated tables. Marshall nevertheless insisted that although McLaurin had not been denied equal facilities in terms of buildings, teachers and expenditures, he *had* been denied equal *opportunities* to learn because of the university's restrictions. These prevented him from mingling freely with other students, Marshall said, and deprived him of the opportunity of comparing notes and exchanging views with his classmates. The Supreme Court ruled that all such restrictions must end immediately. *McLaurin* was a significant victory because states could no longer segregate students *inside* a school. Given this, how could they segregate them by keeping *separate* schools.[12]

On the same day *McLaurin* was handed down, the Supreme Court ruled on a case brought by Houston, Texas mailman Heman Sweatt. Sweatt had sought admission to the University of Texas law school in 1946, and had been turned down because he was black. He brought suit, and during the next four years his case wound its way through four different courts. The University of Texas had been ordered by a district court to either admit Sweatt to its all-white facility or establish a separate one for him at all-black Prairie View A&M within the next six months. In compliance, the school hired two faculty members, rented a few rooms in a nearby Houston office building, and opened the all-new Prairie View A&M Law School. Even though this "school" had no library or even a student body, the university maintained that it had complied with the court order, and the district court agreed. Two thousand University of Texas students did not agree, however, and conducted a demonstration on Sweatt's behalf. The campus newspaper ran an editorial predicting that the "vicious evil" of segregation would soon end "here at Forty Acres." Another student prophesied, "Negroes will enter Texas high schools and grammar schools, and what's more, there won't be any riots."

Thus encouraged, Sweatt took the case to the U.S. Supreme Court. In finding for Sweatt, the court wrote that the separate facilities for whites and blacks were not equal, that the white school possesed

> to a far greater degree those qualities which are incapable of objective measurement but which make for greatness in a law school. Such qualities, to name but a few, include reputation of faculty, experience of administration, position and influence of the alumni, . . . and traditions and prestige. It is difficult to believe that one who had a free choice between these law schools could consider the question close.

Sweatt was an important victory because the Supreme Court now insisted that separate but equal schooling was more than a mere slogan to lip-honor and bandy about. If facilities were to be separate, they must *truly* be *equal* also. It had really meant *Plessy*, the court was saying, and henceforth, equality must be *real* and substantial. It had taken more than a half-century to come just to this point.[13]

But ever since the *Plessy* decision, a small segment of American scholarship had beeen chipping away at the armor of white supremacy. In 1898, William Edward Burghardt Du Bois had written *Philadelphia Negro*, the first major sociological treatise to challenge the idea that vice and crime among urban blacks resulted form their innate moral degeneracy. Economics, not biology, was the culprit here, Du Bois wrote. Du Bois was probably the best educated black scholar in the U.S. at the turn of the century. A *cum laude* graduate of Harvard, he studied two years in Europe and then returned to Harvard for his Ph.D. in 1896. He studied under Max Weber and Rudolph Virchow at the University of Berlin, and under William James and George Santayana at Harvard. In 1903, Du Bois's *Souls of Black Folk* argued that Negroes could contribute much more than mere muscle to building American culture if they were given the chance through education and votes. Taken for granted now, such ideas were "insights" at the beginning of the 20th Century. Since they contradicted established scholarship, they were not readily accepted.

Other works written by black intellectuals and white southern scholars added balance and authority to Du Bois. Indeed, the Carnegie Corporation financed several of these volumes. But for all their wealth of detail, maps, charts, statistical tables, critical analyses, and common good sense, they made only a small impact initially on American scholarship. Even as late as 1946, for example the *Encyclopaedia Britannica* maintained that the Negro's "affinity" for dancing and for "troubled, jumpy, neurotic" music could hardly be attributed to environmental causes alone. Even as late as 1956, two years after the *Brown v. Board* decision, the *Britannica* was still claiming that in certain characteristics Negroes were "closely related to the highest anthropoids," and that they stood on "a lower evolutionary plane that white men." Given suitable training, however, they were capable of becoming craftsmen "of considerable skill, particularly in metal work, carpentry, and carving." At mid-20th Century, the *public* view of black Americans was also based on 19th Century sociology. Even in the nation's capital, blacks had to fake a foreign accent or pretend to be foreigners to get into first-run movies. And World War II black veterans complained that while the German prisoners of war they had guarded had been permitted to eat inside American restaurants, they, the guards, had been required to take their meals in kitchens, out of the public view. These contradictions—in reality and the American ideal—were well-known, even in what are now known as the Third World countries, and indeed, the outrage generated there helped to prompt the Harry S Truman administration's concern for the larger implications of civil rights. The Truman concern is best expressed in a letter written by the U.S. secretary of state, Dec 2, 1952, which found its way into the U.S. Supreme Court deliberations on *Brown v. Board* during 1953 and early 1954:

> The U.S. is under constant attack in the foreign press, over the foreign radio, and in such bodies as the United Nations because of the various practices of discrimination against minority groups in this country. As might be expected, Soviet spokesmen regularly exploit the situation in propaganda against the U.S., both within the United Nations and through radio broadcasts and the press, which reaches all corners of the world. Racial discrimination gives unfriendly governments the most effective kind of ammunition for their propaganda warfare.[14]

Shortly after World War II, Thurgood Marshall believed the time had come to press for full scale desegregation. *Murray, Gaines, Sipuel, McLaurin* and *Sweatt* had eroded the "separate but equal" principle so far as graduate and professional schools and colleges and universities were concerned. Now was the time to press even further—into the public school, lower-level arena. Marshall's strategy was to build a case for the U.S. Supreme Court from several suits in a *variety* of settings. This would make it impossible for the Court to decide on what Margold had called the "narrowest ground possible." Although unique in their particulars, each of these suits would ask the same fundamental question— was segregation *in and of itself* unconstitutional? The issue, at last, would have to be faced squarely. As an opportune beginning, School District No. 22's Board of Education in Clarendon County, South Carolina, aroused the ire of black parents by declining to provide bus transportation for their children the same as it did for white children. When the parents bought a second-hand bus of their own, the board refused even to provide gasoline for it, saying that blacks didn't pay enough taxes to justify the expenditure. The conflict served as an excellent test case when the parents sued (*Briggs v. Elliot*, 1948) not only for equal bus transportation, but equal buildings, books, equipment, faculty salaries, and per-pupil expenditures.[15]

Soon afterward, a Merriam, Kansas housewife became indignant at the sight of a run-down Negro school in nearby South Park. She had passed the school merely by chance while driving her maid home from work. What galled the 30-year-old, white, Esther Brown, more than the dilapidated building, however, was the refusal of the board of education to make any improvements until bonds for the new and modern white school were paid off some 40 years hence (they joked). When Brown then learned that segregation was not legal in Kansas in towns the size of South Park to begin with, her indignation quickly turned into outrage, transforming her into a crusader bent on doing something about the deplorable situation. In speeches first at South Park and then all over the state, she railed against the school's lack of a gymnasium, cafeteria and auditorium; about its unsanitary and smelly earthen privy which served both sexes; about its lack of plumbing and adequate heating and lighting, and about its depressing, run-down condition in general. She organized a boycott at the school and arranged for private lessons for the children so that they wouldn't fall behind in their work. She recruited campaign workers and collected money for legal fees. She spoke at churches and on radio, and when at last enough money had come in to file suit on the school board, she did so.[16]

This stormy victory convinced the NAACP in Kansas that they could build a major test case for presentation to the U.S. Supreme Court. In a matter of months, Topeka welder and part-time minister Oliver Brown (no relation to Esther) was recruited by the association to sue the board of education asking that his daughter be admitted to the town's all-white Sumner Elementary School. Indeed, the times seemed most propitious. Then, black parents in Delaware sued to have their children admitted to newer and better all-white schools closer to their homes than the segregated schools they had been attending. In Washington, D.C., a father sued to enroll his 12-year-old son in the city's new Sousa Junior High School, instead of the 48-year-old all-black school he had been attending. And in Virginia, a 14-year-old student who had called her entire junior high school out on strike to protest overcrowding, agreed to have lawyers bring a suit in her name against the State of Virginia, asking that the state's segregated schools be "abolished forever." All five of these cases—*Bollings, Briggs, Brown, Bulah-Belton* and *Davis*—were originally tried in U.S. district courts, and all came to the U.S. Supreme Court on appeal. Since they all asked the same question, they were consolidated under a single title, *Brown v. Board of Education*, and they were all considered together.[17]

Brown was billed "the case of the century." On one side were Thurgood Marshall and a highly competent team of civil rights lawyers, armed with the testimony of 32 of the nation's top experts in education, sociology, psychology, psychiatry and anthropology. On the other side—favoring continued school segregation—was an even more impressive team of lawyers headed by John W. Davis, one of the ablest and most distinguished constitutional lawyers of his time. The 80-year-old Davis was senior partner in a prestigious Wall Street law firm, a former ambassador to the Court of St. James, and the 1924 Democratic party nominee for President of the United States. He had already argued 139 cases before the U.S. Supreme Court, more than any other lawyer of his time. In him, one scholar wrote, were the "ease, warmth and mellowness of the old South," the traits which had caused King George V to call him the "most perfect gentleman" he had ever known.

In their arguments, Marshall said that government-sanctioned segregation inevitably undermined democratic ideals. He asked the court to rule that constitutional rights belonged to individuals, not to groups; that laws singling out any race were of themselves discriminatory; that individual states could not make laws based soley on race; and that the 14th Amendment required that the laws of all states be the same for whites and blacks. Davis countered by saying that race was the "key to history," that it had been the key for "60

99

centuries," and that the matter of race could never be treated "indifferently." He asked the court to rule that the 14th Amendment had not been intended to do away with school segregation; that states had as much right to classify students according to race as they did by sex or age; and that it was the proper use of a state's police powers to separate races to keep down disturbance and to promote the common good.

To decide these questions and others, the court had to determine whether the generations-old pattern that was all at once tradition, law and social custom was now sufficiently outmoded to reverse a once-valid interpretation of the law. Were laws bearing on the issue kinetic or permanent? In doing so, they had to consider what the practical effects of their ruling likely would be, both in the United States and around the world. The great social debate of the century was thus reduced to its essence.

In ruling out segregation in the nation's public schools, the Supreme Court said that the welfare of society was the law's first reason for being, and that a color hierarchy in American schools was no longer permissible. Segregating black children from others solely on grounds of race, the court wrote (repeating the Sumner argument in *Roberts v. City of Boston* 105 years earlier) affected "their hearts and minds in a way unlikely ever to be undone." It generated feelings of inferiority and it impaired children's ability to learn by lowering morale and ambition, and by instilling defeatist attitudes. Segregation destroyed self-respect and stamped children at an early age with a badge of inadequacy and inferiority. Even if teachers and programs and buildings were all equal, the court wrote, black children *still* received an inferior education, since the very fact of their segregation was a source of personal humiliation.

Moreover (as Sumner had also argued more than a century earlier), white children were also harmed by segregation because they learned to stereotype and to generalize about entire groups of people. Yet they readily could observe the contradictions between the principles of equality they were taught at school, and the actual social conditions that prevailed there. Segregation thus created in their minds a confused set of values. Finally, that system caused massive communication breakdowns in society at large, and created a social climate conducive to violence. For all of these reasons, the court ruled that segregated schools were *inherently* unequal, and that dual educational systems were to be abandoned. In a subsequent statement, the court directed that change take place "with all deliberate speed."[18] The next generation would find that antithetical phrase a Pandora's box of troubles.

Six

[1] For a full account of Sumner's remarks see his *Argument . . . against the Constitutionality of Separate Colored Schools, in the Case of Sarah C. Roberts v. the City of Boston. Before the Supreme Court of Mass., Dec. 4, 1849* (Boston: n.p., 1849). Much of this is quoted in Daniel Calhoun (ed.), *The Educating of Americans: A Documentary History* (Boston: Houghton Mifflin Company, 1969) pp. 333-40. See also Sumner's *Works* (Boston: n.p., 1875) II, pp. 328-72. Ironically, *Roberts* was quickly a dead letter as far as the state of Massachusetts was concerned. The legislature there statutorily desegregated schools in 1855. For *Roberts'* wider significance outside Massachusetts, see Leonard W. Levy and Harlan B. Phillips, "The Roberts Case: Source of the 'Separate But Equal' Doctrine," *American Historical Review* 56 (1951): 510-18.

[2] Robert A. Lefler, "Law of the Land" in *With All Deliberate Speed*, ed. Don Shoemaker (New York: Harper & Brothers, 1957). See also *Roberts v. City of Boston*, 5 Cushing Reports 198 (1849). *State ex. rel. Garnes v. McCann*, 21 Oh. St. 198 (1871); *Ward v. Flood*, 48 Calif. 36 (1874); *Cory v. Carter*, 48 Ind. 327 (1874); *People ex. rel. King v. Gallagher*, 93 N.Y. 438 (1883); and *Lehew v. Brummell*, 103 Mo. 546 (1890).

[3] Harlan had himself once owned slaves. Later his grandson of the same name sat on the 1955 Supreme Court which set the time table for desegregation. The prevalence of the elder Harlan's view affirms Chief Justice Charles Evans Hughes' belief that "a dissent in a court of last resort is an appeal to the brooding spirit of the law, (and) to the intelligence of a future day." For an incisive account of *Plessy*, see C. Vann Woodward's "The Case of the Louisiana Traveler,"

in *Quarrels That Have Shaped The Constitution*, ed. John A. Garraty (New York: Harper & Row, 1962) pp. 145-58.

⁴ *New York Times*, July 24, 1922. This issue and the June 20, 1941 *New York Herald Tribune* contain interesting materials concerning Garland. The latter is an account of the fund's dissolution after 19 years of sponsoring many liberal causes. The fund had been a "godsend," the conservative *Tribune* reported, to a number of "movements espoused by zealous but usually impecunious enthusiasts of political hues ranging from shell-pink to magenta."

⁵ The Garland Fund and Margold stories are in Richard Kluger, *Simple Justice* 2 vols., Book Club edition (New York: Alfred A. Knopf, 1975) 2: 737-79; 823-83. See also 1: 169. Chapter 6 follows Kluger throughout.

⁶ Kluger, *Simple Justice*, p. 164 ff. See also Jack Greenberg, *Citizen's Guide to Desegregation: A Study of Social and Legal Change in American Life* (Boston: The Beacon Press, 1955) p. 58.

⁷ William H. Hastie, "Charles Hamilton Houston 1895-1950" in *Journal of Negro History* 35, No. 4 (July 1950): 355-58.

⁸ Thirty-five years after graduating from Howard, Thurgood Marshall was appointed to the U.S. Supreme Court. At the time of his appointment he had argued 52 cases before the high court, and had won all but eight. For a colorful description of the future justice—who said that he wore life "loose as a garment" and never worried "about nothin' "—see James Poling's "Thurgood Marshall and the Fourteenth Amendment," *Collier's* 129, Part 1 (February 23, 1952): 29 ff.

⁹ Houston called the *Murray* victory a "slight wedge," but cautioned supporters not to "shout too soon." The state could not "tax an entire population for the exclusive benefit of a single class," he wrote, and the "fight has just begun." See his "Don't Shout Too Soon," *Crisis* 43, No. 3 (March 1936): 79 ff. Extensive coverage of *Murray* is in Baltimore's *Afro-American Ledger*, June 22, 1935. *Afro* claimed to be the nation's "biggest colored weekly." See also Kluger *Simple Justice*, pp. 234-44. Missouri's "Lincoln University," by the way, should not be confused with "Black Princeton," Marshall's Pennsylvania alma mater of the same name.

¹⁰ Hill and Greenburg, *Citizen's Guide*, p. 60 and

Kluger, *Simple Justice*, pp. 251-66. Unfortunately, Lloyd Gaines' case did not have the same happy ending as Donald Murray's. Even before his final hearing, Gaines dropped from view, and his whereabouts and the reason for his departure remain a mystery even today. Although he was of draft age, his name did not appear on the World War II draft list. When Gaines failed to take advantage of the court's decision, Missouri set up an all-black law school.

[11] Hugh W. Speer, *The Case of the Century: A Historical and Social Perspective on Brown v. Board of Education*, U.S. Office of Education (DHEW), Document #024747 (Washington: unpublished, 1968) p. 14. In characteristic good humor, Marshall told the district court judge that this new law school had fewer books than the library at the state prison. The "best way for a Negro to get an education in Oklahoma," he noted ironically, "is to go to prison." The judge laughed. See also Kluger, pp. 323-336.

[12] Kluger, *Simple Justice*, pp. 334-57. In the classroom, McLaurin was required to sit at a special desk railed off with a "Reserved for Colored" sign on it. White students soon tore this down and sat with McLaurin in the special unmarked row the regents then reserved for his own exclusive use. Just before *McLaurin* was handed down, Charles Houston, who had collaborated with Marshall 15 years earlier in initiating the desegregation drive, died at the age of 54. Although he did not live to see public school segregation abolished, Houston was eulogized as being "truly the Moses" of the long journey through the "legal wilderness of second class citizenship." See Hastie's "Houston" in *Journal of Negro History* 35, No. 4 (July, 1950): 356-57.

[13] Kluger, *Simple Justice*, pp. 326-57. The case was styled *Sweatt v. Painter*. See also Hill and Greenberg, *Citizen's Guide*, pp. 68-69, 75-76; and Garraty (ed) *Quarrels That Have Shaped the Constitution*, p. 256. Although Sweatt was later dropped from school for poor grades, this denoument in no way changed the case's legal significance.

[14] Quoted in Carl T. Rowan's series of articles titled "Jim Crow's Last Stand," *Minneapolis Morning Tribune*, November 29-December 9, 1953. For Du Bois' education, see his *Autobiography* (New York: International Publishers, 1968) pp. 132-82. See also, Gustavus Myers, *A History of*

Bigotry in the United States, ed. Henry M. Cristman (New York: Capricorn Books, 1960) pp. 461-74.

[15] Per pupil expenditures were decidedly unequal. In 1949, expenditures for whites—who made up only 30% of the population—had been four times that which was spent on blacks. Black schools were typically hardscrabble shanties lacking running water and even sanitary toilets. Textbooks used in black schools had already been worn out in the white schools. One black school in the county didn't even have desks. In another, two earth toilets served 694 pupils. Similar conditions were found in *all* the segregating states. See Speer, *Case of the Century*, pp. 85-108; Kluger, *Simple Justice*, pp. 4-31 and 416-61; and Hill and Greenberg, *Citizen's Guide*, pp. 78-79.

[16] Franklin Williams and Earl Fultz, "The Merriam School Fight," *Crisis* 56, No. 5 (May 1949): 140 ff. Speer, *Case of the Century*, pp. 16-84, and Kluger, *Simple Justice* , pp. 468-534. See also William Barry Furlong, "The Case of Linda Brown," *New York Times*, February 12, 1961.

[17] The Delaware cases *Bulah v. Gebhart* and *Belton v. Gebhart* were considered together when they reached the U.S. Supreme Court. On the D.C. case, *Bolling v. Sharpe*, see Carl F. Hansen, *Danger in Washington: The Story of My Twenty Years in the Public Schools in the Nation's Capital* (West Nyack, New York: Parker Publishing Company, 1968) pp. 1-21. For *Davis v. County School Board of Prince Edward County*, and the five cases as a whole, see Kluger, *Simple Justice*, pp. 540-70, 643-648; and Speer, *Case of the • Century*, pp. 109-148.

[18] For a reconstruction of the court's secret deliberations, see Kluger, *Simple Justice*, 737-39, 823-83. See also James Reston, "A Sociological Decision," *New York Times*, May 18, 1954. This entire issue of the *Times* deals with the background and significance of *Brown*.

SEVEN
For Women: The Longest Battle

"The Americans have done all they could to raise women morally and intellectually to the level of men, and in this respect they appear to have exactly understood the true principle of democratic improvement."

Alexis De Tocqueville
Democracy In America (1835)

While American public education opened a wee crack to admit an increasing number of blacks in the late 19th Century, no substantial accommodation was made for fully one half the white population: females of every age. The implication of a black's inferiority was greatly undermined once he was taken out of the institution that confined him to that debasement. But he was always a *man*, and education was opened to him fundamentally because he could thereby exercise the qualities and talents ascribed to masculinity: strength, endurance, intelligence, stability. No act of Congress, no amendment of Constitution, no judgment of the Supreme Court could remove from women the weaknesses and uselessness ascribed to them for countless centuries.

All the major civilizations predating the Golden Age of Greece assigned subordinate social and educational roles to females. As part of social structures, education reflected these differentiations. Although the earliest Sumerian women were probably polyandrous—suggesting an equal if not dominant social role—the civilization from 3500 B.C. forward was male dominated. Select Sumerian boys were taught government and law in formal schools, while girls learned cooking and child care from their mothers at home.

Well-born Egyptian boys, from 3100 B.C. forward, began their education at 5; but girls, wearing pigtails and playing with dolls, received none except informally at the hands of their mothers. Only the males of the mighty Babylonian and Assyrian civilizations which flourished between 3000 and 1100 B.C. were educated in the literature, religion and medicine of the times, as thousands of extant cuneiform tablets dealing with the daily life and changing customs of the times reveal.

From earliest times, therefore, and with few exceptions, Western females have been regarded as home-makers, ornaments, help-mates and conjugal partners. Almost none received the same kind of education as males, and few participated in the more masculine and weighty affairs of commerce, government and religion. Similarly, the early Eastern civilizations of the Indus and Yellow River valleys, which flourished from 2700 to 1500 B.C. were patriarchal, and females were generally cast in supporting roles.

In both the East and West, religious texts were the unquestioned source of restricted social and educational roles for girls. In establishing the legal code of Hinduism, the prophet Manu commanded that boys and girls be educated separately and differently; the former in the classics and laws, the latter in household arts. Girls were "delicate and precious," Manu proclaimed, and should be treasured and protected and "kept in dependence" by the males of their families "both night and day." The Hebrew prophet Moses, credited with writing the *Pentateuch*, believed that God had commanded women to submit both to their husbands' affections and to their rule. Indeed, throughout most of the *Old Testament*, virtuous women are portrayed as being submissive to men and supportive of them. The ideal wife, King Solomon wrote, worked to the advantage of her husband, satisfied all his needs and never hindered him. Only the male children of Solomon's time were educated in the *Torah* or the laws. This Judaist idea of female subordination in educational and social matters carried forward into the early Christian church. Although Jesus as founder had seemed to dignify women as full persons, thereby attracting large numbers of them to his movement, he made no explicit call for their social parity. Nor did Paul, who organized the early church. Indeed, Paul's views on women were entirely traditional, and his writings tended to set women off as an inferior and dependent class. Likewise, formative Buddhism, Confucianism, and Islam stressed female subjugation. Sexual codes were double-sided, and although strict constraints were placed on women, few were imposed upon men. Concubinage and polygamy were condoned or routinely forgiven. Females, in fact, were so inferior, Gautama believed, that they were incapable of reaching the higher grades of holiness unless first reborn into some other form. Confucius required wives to obey their husbands *and* their husbands' parents. And Mohammed, and probably his 12 wives and three concubines as well, beleived that in Paradise men would be waited upon by beautiful sloe-eyed virgins called *houris*. With each religion, substantive education was a male prerogative. Boys were educated in the laws and the classics—and girls, separate and apart, were trained in the domestic and household arts.[1]

Much of the non-sacred literature of antiquity also shows a male bias and male orientation. In his *History of Animals*, Aristotle had noted that females by nature were "more jealous, querulous, prone to despondency, more apt to scold and strike, more deceptive and false of speech, more void of shame and self-respect, and more shrinking and difficult to rouse to action." Males, by their natures, Aristotle believed were "more spirited, more savage, more simple, more hopeful and less cunning." Even among lower animals, "nature makes a differentiation in the mental characteristics of the two sexes." Males are "more courageous than females, and more sympathetic in the way of standing by to help," he declared. Thus, in the animal kingdom, the "male is superior and the female inferior; the one rules and the other is ruled." Of necessity, this principle of male predominance "extends to all mankind," the "true intentions of nature" being revealed in the behavior of lower species. In the human family as in the animal kingdom, "the male is by nature fitter for command than the female." In sum, females were nothing but "misbegotten males." Because Aristotle's writings were second only to the Bible as influences on

English social thought, his dogmas were deemed fundamental.

The position of women was only sometimes improved in the old world. Athenian women reached a high point when Plato recommended their equal education with men. Spartan women were even "more equal" in that they owned about 40 per cent of the city's real estate. And the position of Roman women was advanced further still. Nonetheless, the old world was a *man's* world, and while conditions for women were here and there improved beyond the norm, they were nowhere fully equal.[2]

In the Middle Ages, Thomas Aquinas wrote that if God had intended women to govern, Eve would have been created from Adam's head, not his rib. Reflecting a more enlightened age's questioning, Shakespeare's Katharina condemned women who sought "supremacy and sway" when they were bound to "serve, love and obey." With similar satire, Cervantes' Lothario declared women imperfect animals needful of chivalrous conduct on the part of men. Going beyond satire to social criticism, Jonathan Swift's Captain Lemuel Gulliver, discoverer of Houyhnhnm Island, found female Yahoos there possessed of the same "lewdness, coquetry, censure and scandal" found universally and "by instinct in womankind." Girls should be educated equally with boys, a Houyhnhnm told Gulliver. Otherwise, half the population would be "good for nothing but bringing children into the world." And to trust the care and training of children to such useless animals, the Houyhnhnm declared, would be a "great instance of brutality."[3] Did the full blown Age of Enlightenment build on Swift's clear thinking? One of its greatest philosophers, Jean Jacques Rousseau, called females "the sex which ought to obey." The whole education of girls, he wrote, "ought to be relative to men, to please men, to be useful to them, and to make their lives sweet and agreeable." Rousseau's *Emile* prescribed quite a different kind of education for boys. Dr. Samuel Johnson, remembered for his prejudices and personality, was aghast that women should enter into the ministry, and agreed with James Boswell, his biographer, that the sexes would probably never be equal, "even in heaven." Yet, Johnson believed that women would be "none the worse" for a man's education, even though the idea ran counter to "the common notion." For Boswell's part, it was enough that women be "sensible and well-informed;" it was far too much that they be educated the same as men. The subsequent Age of Industry was, of course, a reaction to the humanist optimism of the 18th Century. Although its principal philosopher, Charles Darwin, was a grandson of a ranking English feminist, he believed males to be clearly superior to females in matters requiring "deep thought, reason and imagination." Whatever men took up, he wrote, whether science, history or philosophy, they clearly attained "a higher eminence" than women.

It was argued that schools would harden and deform girls and make them unattractive and unmarriageable, militating against the home and family. It would come to race suicide, many complained, if girls should become so independent that they had no need to marry and produce children. An educated woman would be disrespectful to her husband, it was believed, and no man with even a semblance of pride could long tolerate an "uppity" woman. They would refuse to do housework, and turn their children over to schools as babysitters.

Physically, it was believed that girls' brains were "too light, their foreheads too small, their reasoning powers too underdeveloped, and their emotions too easily worked upon to make serious students." Girls had a certain amount of "superficial cleverness," it was widely agreed, and they could "pick up" a little of almost any subject. But they were far too shallow to go into anything very far. Intellectually, they were not up to the mark. But even if they could pass their courses, their health would fail in the process; girls simply could not study as many hours per day as boys could. They could not be put through the same rigorous intellectual course as boys; they would die in the process. And even should some survive the training, the intellectual rigor would make them harsh and competitive, when in fact they were meant to be soft and submissive. Finally, on physical grounds, the most competent medical authority stated that female study would impede the milk supply of mothers and interfere with their nursing capabilities. The philosopher, Hubert Spenser, wrote that strenuous study might even cause infertility in women.[4]

Even at the beginning of the present century, G. Stanley Hall, one of the foremost scholars of his day and founder of the child studies disciplines, opposed co-education of the sexes in American high schools. "Bookishness is a bad sign in girls" he wrote, and "suggests artificiality." Indeed, co-education might make boys effeminate and "attract them out of their orbit," and it could "functionally castrate girls" and cause them to "lose pride in their sex," and lapse into "mannish ways and ideals." In any case, girls were weaker, especially during menstruation, Hall believed, and might not bear up under the strain of a male education. They should not "pluck the apple of intelligence at too great a cost of health," the eminent Harvard professor and university president wrote. Accordingly, Hall recommended a "humanistic and liberal" education for girls focusing primarily on "wifehood and motherhood." Certainly chemistry and physics were "too complex" for females and should be kept "at the elementary stages," he wrote. Zoology should be taught with plenty of pet animals, and botany should emphasize flowers and gardening. Again, Latin and Greek were too complicated, but conversational dinner French was not. And in no case should girls be trained to independence and self support. In fact, Hall wrote, "excessive intellectualism . . . instills an aversion to brute maternity," and this could doom the race to extinction, much the same as the celibacy of early Christian monks (an elite intelligentsia leaving no posterity) contributed to the arrival of the Dark Ages. The only advantage to coeducation—if indeed there was one—Hall wrote, accrued to boys. For they would probably study harder to out-score the girls, and their conduct, in the presence of girls, would probably be more refined.[5]

Early support for female education began in England during the 17th Century. One of the first to speak out— although she expected "many scoffes and taunts from inconsiderate and illiterate men," she wrote—was Bathusa Pell Makin, one-time tutoress to Elizabeth, daughter of Charles

I. Ladies of leisure and intelligence should be granted full educational opportunities with men, Makin wrote in 1673. No public or social use would be made of their education, she assured her readers, for indeed God had "made man the head." Instead, the purpose of women's education would be to polish their souls and make them better help-mates to their husbands. Learned women would not be overbearing or "impudent." Even men stood much to gain from female education, Makin wrote; for men, becoming "ashamed of their own ignorance," would take up studies themselves so as not to be outdone by the weaker sex. Why should women settle for the curling iron and fashion, she asked, when they could become "philosophers, poets and mathematicians."[6]

Twenty years after her, Daniel Defoe condemned the "inhuman" and "barbarous" custom of denying the advantages of learning to girls. What had they done, he asked, to forfeit the privilege of education; and how could girls, taught only to read and write, even hope to converse intelligently at the dinner table? Was any *man* so artificially educated ever good for anything, he asked. And how could men, who denied learning to women in the first place, even be attracted to such ignorant creatures? Men need not fear competition from women, Defoe wrote, for learned women would no more encroach upon the prerogatives of men than men of sense would oppress the weakness of women. "All the world are mistaken" about educating women, Defoe wrote. For he could not believe that God made such "delicate, glorious, creatures . . . to be only stewards, cooks and slaves."[7]

About the same time, Mary Astell, a London essayist, complained that although much time, care and expense were given to the education of boys, girls were given little or none. Indeed, boys had "every imaginable encouragement," she wrote in 1697; and by their education they gained "title, authority, power and riches." Yet, girls, whose minds were equally worth training, were driven from the "tree of knowledge" by the "never-failing scarecrow of laughter and ridicule." A special school for girls was needed, Astell wrote. Owing to the temper of the times, however, her proposal came to naught.[8]

Early in the 18th Century, Philip Stanhope, the fourth

Earl of Chesterfield, expressed the wisdom of the times regarding women in a letter dated September 5, 1748. "Women . . . are only children of a larger growth," he wrote. "They have an interesting tattle and sometimes wit; but for solid reasoning good sense, I never . . . knew one that had it, or who reasoned or acted intelligently for four and twenty hours together." A man "of sense only trifles with them, plays with them, humors and flatters them, as he does with a child," the Earl wrote, and he "neither consults them . . . nor trusts them with serious matters; though he . . . makes them believe that he does . . . for they love mightily to be dabbling in business which they always spoil."[9]

Later in that century, Mary Wollstonecraft produced *Vindication of the Rights of Women,* a work whose influence on the history of women has yet to be equaled. Writing at the time of the French Revolution, which she feared would not materially alter the position of women, Wollstonecraft condemned the practice of educating girls only in the "miscalled accomplishments." Among the more popular of those were subjects like music, dance, reading, art, conversational French and Italian, writing, needlework, and works of travel and poetry. Only a few of the better women's schools permitted more than "a peep" at the barest outlines of mathematics, science and language. (One tongue was quite enough for a woman, it was claimed.) The accomplishments, Wollstonecraft wrote, mutilated the "mind and spirit," and reduced girls to the role of sexual beings and kept them in a state of "specious innocence" and "perpetual childhood." Indeed, the trivial attentions and "regal homage" men heaped upon women (attending to doors, picking up handkerchiefs, etc.), only "insultingly support(ed)" their own superiority. As long as women were beguiled by such "ludicrous ceremonies" which seemed to exalt, but really degraded them, they would continue to live in a state of "gilded slavery." Furthermore, a national system of co-education catering to the middle and lower classes—and not to "ladies" only—was needed, she argued, so that women could be taught to be "rational wives" instead of "alluring mistresses."

How much better to converse with men as friends and

equals, thereby challenging them to higher, more noble thoughts, than to seek to "impress" them by watching to turn an apt French expression, or work in some obscure line of Greek poetry. Indeed, educated women could rid themselves of their "gay and giddy" stereotype and stamp out the old humbug linking femininity and frailty by which women had so long been given to swooning and delicate health. Why labor "to be weaker than nature intended," she asked, when muscular strength, the main source of male superiority, had long been renounced by men themselves as inimical to the character of a gentleman.

But if Wollstonecraft only mildly condemned the flim-flam of 18th Century convention regarding women, she roundly denounced sexist intellectuals like Rousseau, the Reverend James Fordyce, and Lord Chesterfield. Rousseau was only a "learned pig," she wrote, whose imagination had "run wild." How his "mighty sentiments" were lowered when he spoke of women, and how "puerile" were his ob-servations that modest school girls had a natural delicacy about writing the letter "O;" or that girls, by nature, were fonder of dolls, dreaming and talking than boys. Such "ridi-culous stories" were "below contempt," she wrote, and they did not merit "serious refutation." Neither would Wollstonecraft have girls read the sermons of Dr. Fordyce since they depicted virtuous women as being little more than "house slaves." Such "sentimental rantings" were "indecent and disgusting," she wrote, and indeed they entirely moved her gall. Chesterfield's views on women were "unmanly, frivolous and immoral," she declared.

A remarkably liberated woman for her time, Mary Wollstonecraft did not fit into the conventional mold of 18th Century womanhood. Indeed, she rejected fashion, accom-plishments "undue adornment," chivalry, ballroom cour-tesies and belittling patronage, and her message was that women were more than frail barks on a storm-tossed sea. They could take charge of their lives, she believed, and refuse to be pets or clinging vines inspiring only paternal and degrading epithets like "baby" and "doll." With edu-cation, they could change the "kiss me and be quiet" at-titudes of men, and gain happiness, self-mastery and financial independence, never again being reduced to "pocket searching" for miscellaneous expenses. Wollstonecraft declared war on every cliche of her day. It was *not* clever of girls to pretend ignorance in the company of boys; it was *not* masculine to want a male education; and education would *not* lower a woman's charm value, nor would it diminish her capacities as a mother. Written in just three months, *Rights of Women* created a sensation in Europe and the United States, and gave Wollstonecraft world-wide fame and recognition. Perhaps because it was dismissed out of hand by conservatives along with many of the other "revolutionary" ideas of the time, it worked with slow effect.[10]

Two other English writers influenced the movement that led to the education of girls in the United States. Hannah More, one of the most learned women of her time, except for the subjects of Latin and mathematics (which her father would not permit her to study, believing they would cause her headaches), called for "solid" and challenging studies for girls in her *Strictures on Female Education*, published in 1799.

Nothing was so "deadening to the mind and soul," she wrote, as the so-called "accomplishments," and only a rigorous boys' curriculum could help girls to learn to "methodize, think and compare." An education was not intended to change the "place" of girls, however. Indeed, More was horrified at the very idea of sexual equality, and she often boasted of her refusal to even read Wollstonecraft's *Rights of Women*. In admitting the inferiority of her own sex, More's views were strictly in keeping with her times. But in founding some of the best girls' schools in England, and in insisting that both sexes be permitted to attend Sunday Schools for the poor—which she took a hand in founding, and which later became a large enterprise in the United States—her work was considerably advanced beyond her own time.[11]

Erasmus Darwin, grandfather of Charles Darwin, and a poet, inventor and philosopher in his own right, provided another stimulus to girls' eduation with the simultaneous publication in London and Philadelphia in 1798 of *A Plan for the Conduct of Female Education*. Darwin's plan was one of the first to call for rigorous *scientific* study, and also vocational studies, for girls. As future mothers, females should educate themselves so as to be able to step in and provide for their families in the event of their husbands' "inactivity, folly or death." Darwin had his own two daughters—for whom he saw problems because of their illegitimacy—educated along these lines, and then placed them in charge of a school conducted according to the plan. Unlike Wollstonecraft, Darwin had no interest in educating girls for their future emancipation, but only for their personal development and possible later stand-by use. Education, he wrote, should instill in girls the "mild and retiring" virtues, as opposed to the "bold and dazzling" ones, and it should reinforce the "youthful timidity" and "blushing embarrassment" of young girls, these being, he wrote, "the most powerful of their charms." Darwin did not intend that girls be given a *full* boys' education. But his plan came closer to providing one than any other plan then proposed.[12] But the prevailing sentiment in the United States at this time still took its inspiration from John Winthrop, the first governor of Massachusetts. Winthrop had written that a "godly young woman" of his acquaintance had suffered a nervous breakdown because she had given "herself wholly to reading and writing." Had she attended "to her household affairs," the governor wrote, "and such things as are proper to women, she might have kept her wits." With the development of the concept of gentility in the early Victorian period, such objections to female learning gave way to a new set of objections; namely, that education would coarsen girls and render them masculine and unmarriageable.[13]

But the rise of an entirely new class of working women in America was more important than any of the foregoing writers in the educational emancipation of women. The rise of industrial manufacturing changed the basic fabric of everyday life for virtually the entire country. Power looms, for example, gave rise to a new textile industry, and removed the production of clothing from home to factory. Increasingly, women's handiwork was done by machine and increasingly women and adolescent girls moved to large cities, where factories located to take advantage of power and cheap labor supplies. As young girls were exploited in the mills and sweatshops of the period—northern capitalists were making more from hireling labor, it was said, than southern planters were making from their slaves-the traditional view of women as delicate flowers fit only for hearth and home could not long survive. In effect, the position of women changed from that of a parasitic class, which was generally *acceptable* to men, to that of a vast oppressed vassalage, which was *unacceptable*—particularly to men socialized in Victorian ethics, i.e., possessed of gallant and chivalrous instincts. It did little for their idealized view of girls as "graceful creatures" to watch them shovel coal in 160-degree heat at the smelting plant, naked from the waist up, or to see young women grow old before their time working 80-hour weeks, and often falling asleep at their machinery in the mills of the day. Indeed, education came to be seen as a means by which girls and women might obtain more "gentle" employment. An increasingly large number of men came to see education as a means by which girls could escape the degredation of this new serfdom, and also as a means by which they could hold on to or regain their natural femininity and womanhood. Whereas the view had been that education would coarsen girls, it came to be that education would reinforce and strengthen their femininity. A far greater number of men began to look at female education in a softer light on moral grounds. From the factory, it seemed but one step down to prostitution. Lust, many claimed, was a "better paymaster than the garment manufacturer: Why labor for pennies when a smile will buy a nice supper?" The specter of prostitution undoubtedly helped the cause of women's education.

At first, a few schools admitted girls for an hour's instruction before and after school, while the boys were away. Others paid teachers a small additional fee to teach girls during the boys' lunch hour, or on Thursday afternoons, which was then a holiday from school. Still others admitted girls to studies from 5 until 7 in the morning during the summer months—May through September—while most boys were away on harvest or vacation. Some schools simply gave the long term to boys and the short summer term to girls. Finally, by mid-century, a few girls were attending schools at the same times and in the same buildings as boys, but still usually in different rooms. If conditions required that a single room be shared, boys sat on one side and girls the other.[14] But usually rooms and teachers were different; and usually girls were taught in inverse proportion to a subject's true importance. Music and dancing were the subjects most emphasized for girls, while the boys' forte— Latin and mathematics—were hardly emphasized at all. Girls copied pencil drawings, memorized poetry, and studied some of the rules of grammar, but in the latter case, emphasis was superficially placed on the exceptions to the rules. Very slowly, the traditional views concerning girls and education began to change, and imperceptibly, the place and position of women began to change. Personal loveliness came to mean something more than grace at pouring tea, or kindness, obedience, loyalty and usefulness. It came to embrace to a small extent the qualities of intellect and reason. Learning need not be acquired at the expense of femininity, many came to believe; and it was not necessarily assertive, mannish or uppity or conceited for women to want to develop their intellects beyond the point of mere literacy.[15]

Because the old grammar schools were in a state of transition from secondary to elementary schools, girls' education remained basic and rudimentary; any who wanted secondary schooling had to attend the few female academies, seminaries and normal schools that were available. The earliest high schools had excluded girls. Even when Boston opened a separate high school for girls, it was closed for lack of interest. But increasingly after the Civil War, high schools began to admit girls, especially those in the large cities; by the end of the century about half the grammar schools in the country educated boys and girls together, in the same rooms at the same times and under the same teachers. But beyond grammar schools of seven or eight year's duration, and beyond high schools of two, three or four years' duration, Americans opposed collegiate education for "girls"—the word "girls" was correct usage because the admission age to college was usually only 14 or 15.

Here, at the collegiate level, men drew the line. Indeed, many complained, it was difficult to imagine that a girl could be so self-destructive as to want a man's *real* (higher) education. They simply would not hear of co-education at the undergraduate level. But a few women began attempts to by-pass undergraduate education altogether and break into graduate and professional schools for the learned processions—education, medicine, law and the Christian ministry. (The same tack—breaking into graduate schools in advance of undergraduate schools—would be taken by blacks a century later as they pressed for higher education.) At this level, it was believed, oppositon would be minimal. Instead, the outcry was very loud. When Elizabeth Blackwell applied for admission to a medical school in the 1840's, the entire medical profession was aghast. What woman of modesty would even suggest such an indecency? What proper woman could ask men to remove their clothing for a physical examination? (The reverse situation was, of course, acceptable.) Any man would rather go untreated than submit to a female examination. What man would stoop to hire such a woman? The study of the human body was not a fit study for a woman of refinement. It would bring impure thoughts to her mind, and her presence both in the classroom and in the examination room would unnecessarily stimulate both sexes. As a compromise, most women candidates for medical school agreed that they would only treat other women and children below the age of puberty.

Men doctors also feared that women would over-populate the medical profession and thereby destroy it. No one would hire a woman doctor, not knowing if she could be depended upon in an emergency since her own home naturally came first. Home duties were bound to interfere with a medical practice, many concluded. Women should stick with the Bible which had not recommended them beyond the nursing and midwifery roles. Medical societies, hospitals and medical schools agreed that such professional education would destroy women's delicate feelings and refined sensibilities.

Leaning against these blasts, Blackwell obtained a medical degree in 1849. She was admitted to a small medical school in Geneva, New York. But when a woman applied for admission to Harvard Medical School in 1850, officials refused on the grounds that neither students nor faculty were ready for such a move. Johns Hopkins at Baltimore became the first major university to admit women to medical school on the same basis as men.

Similarly, spokesmen for the legal profession claimed that women could never master the complicated subject of law; there was a vast difference in the sexes as to the ability to apply and understand legal principles. How could women practice law when they themselves were dead in the law? (The legal existence of a wife was suspended during marriage at the time, so that in most states she could not make a will, sue or be sued in her own name, nor could she inherit property, control her earnings or sign legal papers.) Moreover, a woman's duties were incompatible with public life. The law dealt with coarse, brutal and repulsive affairs, and was therefore not a proper calling for women. Even worse, with legal training women would be able to manage men's property, and they would soon teach other women how to become financially independent of men. This could destroy marriage, the home and the family.

Lawyers expressed the exclusionism of all professions. Why take a law degree, they demanded, when there still was no chance of being admitted to the bar (the contracts of married women were not binding.)

Women would be too merciful and too lenient with criminals; once trained in law they could clamor to become judges, sheriffs, even governors. The line had to be drawn somewhere. Not until 1870 did Ada Keply become the first woman graduate of an American law school, the Union College of Law in—notably—the booming, polyglot industrial city of Chicago, in 1870. After much more contention, other schools permitted women to attend law school lectures but not graduate, then to graduate but not be admitted to the bar, then to be admitted to the bar but restricted in this or that way in their practices. Finally, in 1918, Yale University opened its law school doors (only) to women: this was followed in 1920 by the University of Virginia, and by others thereafter.

Not surprisingly, the profession most opposed to the admission of women to its schools was the Christian ministry. Methodism's founder, John Wesley, considered it a scandal for a woman to preach, and even Anne Hutchinson, a religious leader in colonial America, had been banished from the church by men who considered her and her doctrines heretical. Quaker women had always preached, but this was a minor sect. Did not the Bible speak clearly on the subject?, preachers intoned. Many women answered these admonitions by pointing out that there was no Biblical justification for the inferior position of women, that the scriptures were not necessarily divine in every case, and that they necessarily reflected the agricultural, patriarchal society which had produced them. *True* respect of women did not entail bowing and scraping, but rather respecting them as full persons. If men were *truly* noble, they said, they would raise the position of women, not keep them pinned to the ground with dirty boots. Preachers reminded women that Paul had admonished, "Let your women keep silent in the churches." Women should cleave to the church-related work customarily available to them: mission and social work, teaching, religious and music education, and even as deaconesses in some instances. Women would have to devote so much of their time overcoming public opposition to their presence in the pulpit that there would be no energy left for God's work.

By the late 1840's, some women were admitted to theological seminaries as special students. First, they could take courses by not degrees, then they could take degrees but not be ordained, then they could be ordained, but preach only if they could find a congregation willing to accept them. Antoinette Brown was the first woman to graduate from a theological school in the United States: at Oberlin College in 1851. The first school to open to women on the same basis as men was Hartford Theological Seminary in 1884.

Only seldom did women graduates in any of the professions find work; when they did work, the pay was less than half what their male counterparts earned. If women graduates found work, and subsequently married, they usually gave up their professional lives, on the principal— agreed to by both sexes—that no married woman should take bread from the mouth of man. On economic grounds it therefore seemed senseless to many that a girl should spend $3,000 on a college education, then graduate and marry at 17 or 18, and find the expensive education useless. With that same $3,000, it was argued, a woman could hire a servant girl for the first four or five years of her marriage—the critical years—and thereby concentrate *all* her energies on fulfilling her *true* role—catering to the physical and other needs of her husband and children. In cold economic terms, a girl's college education was a needless extravagance, a waste of time and money. Indeed, to even think of such an education was selfish and egotistical, and the last word sometimes carried with it a connotation of questionable sexual preference. Some feared a rise in crime—owing to a decrease in the mother's care and influence over her children—if women were educated. *Ordinary* men would certainly be hurt, many protested in that educated women would refuse to marry them. And the loss of financial support from philanthropists (many of whom opposed female education to the last breath) would cause many closings in colleges for both men *and* women, it was widely acknowledged. Finally, it was feared, with education women would next be wanting the vote. And then what?

Some of the strongest objections to female education came from men who thought the movement was "anti-man" in its motivation. It wounded their dignity that what women were really objecting to was the patriarchal family, the kind sanctioned in the Bible. A coming matriarchy was predicted, and this would completely explode the husband's conjugal authority. Education would destroy romance, it was said; it would compromise a woman's femaleness and lead to disillusionment. It would lessen a girl's conjugal attractions, lead to an irregular sex life, and cause both men and women to lose their mutual dependence upon the other. It might even become necessary for American men to send to Europe for their wives, wrote Dr. Edward H. Clarke of the Harvard Medical faculty in 1873. In sum, girls differed from boys in their tastes, games, family relations and occupations. So why should schools seek to wipe out that distinction.[16]

By their upbringing most women agreed with these views, or at least dared not object to them. Others reasoned mildly that it did not seem right that God should make girls natural, full and talented, and that they should then look only to the home as the major source of their identity. A restructuring of the school and the place of work was called for, they said, so that in the absence of social compulsion, they could help to build a better world.

The talents of women were, of course, best observed in the classroom; teaching was therefore the easiest of the professions to break into. Still, there were drawbacks. According to *Harper's Magazine* (1878), "when a young woman commences to teach, she loses nine chances in 10 for marriage. If she teaches five years, her chances for marriage are but one in 100; and if she teaches 10 years, her chances for marriage and good social position are but one in 10,000."[17] Still, anything was better than wage-slavery at the mill or factory. And if men would just think about it, the co-education of boys and girls could work advantageously for both sexes. They lived together as brothers and sisters, after all, and later on as husbands and wives. So why should they be artificially separated in matters of schooling?

Coeducation thus seemed to be an acceptable compromise. Marriage partners-to-be could take the measure of each other in school. Marriages could be more reciprocal, with neither sex owning or dominating the other. Boys *and* girls could obtain a more balanced or "symmetrical" view of questions under study. And discipline should improve with the co-education of the sexes; and costs should go down since it was doubly expensive to maintain a dual set of schools. Increasingly in the late 19th Century, co-education in high schools and colleges came to be seen as normal, natural, economical, convenient, and judicious—and of positive benefit to *both* sexes.

The next step was to let women have their own *programs* (just as blacks could have their own *schools*), with the idea that it would preoccupy them and would forestall greater ambitions. Indeed, there were many kinds of higher education, conservatives began to say, and college girls need not always pursue the same *courses* as boys. An entirely new course of studies (now called "home economics") was then introduced into the colleges that women were beginning to attend. New courses in child care, cooking, sewing, and budget-making were justified in that they could not help but improve home life and elevate the housewife beyond the menial or the factory worker. Men trained for their various trades and professions, so why should women not be as well trained for theirs? And if these homemaking courses siphoned off a number of women from the learned professions—well, after all, it *was* a free country. As soon as such courses were well-established on college campuses, they began to trickle down into the secondary or high schools. The Chicago public school system put in a home-making course in 1898; other school systems followed. A little later "commercial" subjects (typing, shorthand, book-keeping) were added, as were physical education subjects, and it was not uncommon for teachers to advise college-bound girls to take more physical education courses and not "throw the whole force of education upon the brain." The ultimate expression of this separate but equal reasoning was the establishment of women's colleges which did not admit men. Among these were Vassar, Smith, Wellesley, Bryn Mawr, Mt. Holyoke and Randolph-Macon, and all appeared on the scene during the 30-year period, 1861-1891. All had high admissions standards, all attracted top-rate faculty, and all were handsomely endowed. The minimum age requirement was 14. These schools came into being because even in the late 1850's, major American universities, such as Harvard, Columbia and Yale had little good to say for co-education. The president of Harvard had stated that "an immense preponderance of enlightened public opinion" was against the college co-educational experiment; and the president of Yale could see "no possible use" for a college degree for a girl. (Keeping the sexes apart at night would require "constant, sleepless vigilance" another president feared.) Girls simply were not welcome at the major universities. But as a compromise, Harvard did permit some of its professors to leave on their own time and hold classes for a few girls, who except for their sex, met all of Harvard's other admissions requirements. Parents of these students insisted that the instruction be *exactly* the same in terms of amount and quality as that which was available to boys at Harvard.

They would have no watered-down courses or textbooks. In time this unofficial affiliate school came to be called "the annex." No degrees were awarded, but the annex did confer a certificate of attendance, and it did state in writing that the recipient had pursued a course of study equivalent to that for which the B.A. was conferred at Harvard. Finally, in 1893, the annex gained an offical Harvard endorsement as Radcliffe College, named in honor of Harvard's first woman benefactor whose gift in 1641 had got the school through an especially bad winter. Radcliffians—inevitably sweetened to "Cliffies" by Harvard boys—had access to the Harvard Library, located just across the Cambridge Common. The school's degrees were countersigned by the president of Harvard, and he and the Fellows of Harvard served as trustees of the new school. And no faculty members were employed at Radcliffe without the consent of the Harvard Board. Finally, in 1943, Harvard itself was opened to girls.

Harvard did not pioneer in this breakthrough, however, The same pattern developed at Columbia in New York City with a female affiliate, Barnard College, in 1890; and at Tulane University in New Orleans with Sophie Newcomb in 1887. Sophie took only white girls, 14 years of age or older, who had attended grammar school. While female and affiliate colleges presented a rigorous curriculum to their students, none neglected to cultivate the female graces whenever and wherever possible. The mission, goals and purposes of these institutions are perhaps best summed up in the Randolph-Macon *Catalog* for the 1925-26 school year.

> "We wish to establish in Virginia a college where our young women may obtain an education equal to that given in our best colleges for young men, and under environments in harmony with the highest ideals of womanhood; where the dignity and strength of fully developed faculties and the charm of the highest literary culture may be acquired by our daughters without loss to woman's crowning glory—her gentleness and grace."

These affiliate colleges were half-way houses between women's colleges and the modern-day co-educational colleges and universities, so much a part of American life. Almost all the affiliate and women's schools had preparatory departments to offer a kind of compensatory education to their students, since few girls arrived at college as well-prepared as boys. They simply had not received a good enough secondary education to pass a rigorous "man's curriculum." The affiliate colleges helped break down the prejudices of many professors who thought they would be obliged to water down their courses if girls were admitted to them. The majority of professors fought co-education to the bitter end. Women were "divinely endowed with the faculty for seeing only their own side," open professor said. And another complained that because of their "passion for side issues," they would always be getting professors off the subject.

But these were only beginnings. The most appalling evidence testifying to the persistency of inertia were statistics for 1980: only 9% of all doctors and lawyers were women; only 2% judges; 3% dentists, and less than 2% chemists, engineers or physicists. College educated women earned $7,000 less than men with a similar education, and $1,700 less than a man with only a high school diploma. The vast majority of women were still confined to "pink collar" jobs—teachers, typists, cashiers, nurses, bookkeepers, etc.[18] Far more meaningfully than black Americans, the nation's women can chorus, "How long, Oh Lord, how long?"

Seven

[1] Max Muller (ed.) *Sacred Books of the East* (Delhi: Motilal Banarsidass, 1970), v. XXV, pp. 327-28; 75-83. See also Leonard Swidler, *Women in Judaism* (Metuchen, New Jersey: The Scarecrow Press, 1976) pp. 31,114.

[2] Evelyn and Frank Stagg, *Women in the World of Jesus* (Philadelphia: The Westminster Press, 1978) p. 255; and Rosemary Radford Reuther, *Religion and Sexism in the Jewish and Christian Traditions* (New York: Simon and Schuster, 1974) pp. 41-88, 117-49. See also Genesis 3:16; Proverbs 31; I Corinthians 11:1-16 and 14:35; Ephesians 5:22; Colossians 3:18; I Timothy 2:11-12; and I Peter 3:1.

Women should be quiet, sensible and humble, Paul wrote, and they should praise, honor and deeply respect their husbands. Women should not express their views publicly, and they should fit into their husbands' plans and willingly submit to their leadership. If wives have any questions, Paul wrote, they should ask their husbands. For the position of Grecian and Roman women see Plato's *Republic* V, and Aristotle's *Politics* II, 6, 9, 11. See also James Donaldson, *Woman: Her Position and Influence in Ancient Greece and Rome* (New York: Longmans, 1907) p. 120 ff. Aristotle's view that even male and female fish differed in their mental characteristics (males stood by to help females caught on fishing spears, whereas when males were struck, females swam away in fear) is in his *History of Animals*, Book IX, Chapter I. Aristotle's belief that the "intentions of nature" are found in the behavior of lower species is in his *Politics*, Book I, Chapter V.

³ See *City of God*, Book XIX, Chapter 14; *Summa Theologica*, Part I, Question 92; *Taming of the Shrew*, Act V, Scene II; *Don Quixote*, Part I, Chapter 33; and *Gulliver's Travels*, Part IV, Chapters 7, 8. None of Shakespeare's women were educated. Even Portia in his *Merchant of Venice* described herself as an "unlettered girl, unschooled, unpracticed."

⁴ Whatever women wished to do, Rousseau wrote, they should contrive to have their husbands order them to do it. Such views, by modern standards, contradicted his egalitarian ideals. See Rousseau's *On Inequality* and *On Political Economy* in Robert M. Hutchins (ed.) *Great Books of the Western World* (Chicago: William Benton, 1952) v. 38, pp. 319, 346, 367-68. See also Rousseau's *L'Emile*, ed. W. H. Payne (New York: 1906) p. 263. See also in the Hutchins' series, *Life of Johnson*, v. 44, pp. 132, 165, 391; and *Descent of Man*, v. 49, p. 566. It apparently did not occur to Darwin that men reached a "higher eminence" in history and science because these subjects *were not taught to women*. Darwin had no female classmates at Cambridge or Edinburgh.

⁵ G. Stanley Hall, *Adolescence* (New York: D. Appleton and Co., 1905; reprint ed., New York: Arno Press and the *New York Times*, 1969), v. II, pp. 609, 622-646.

6 Parents should see to the education of their daughters and they should not worry that men would not "adventure to marry" them just because they were educated, Makin wrote. See her "Essay to Revive the Ancient Education of Gentlewomen" (1673) in Myra Reynold's *The Learned Lady in England, 1650-1760* (Boston: Houghton Mifflin Co., 1920) pp. 276-86.

7 See Defoe's "Essay on Projects" (1692) in Henry Morley (ed.) *The Earlier Life and Works of Daniel Defoe* (London: George Routledge & Sons, 1889) pp. 144-52. For other indications of Defoe's sympathies with women, see his *Conjugal Lewdness or Matrimonial Whoredom: A Treatise Concerning the Use and Abuse of the Marriage Bed*, reproduced from a copy in the British Museum. (Gainesville, Florida: Scholars' Facsimilies & Reprints, 1967) pp. 379-406. Defoe wrote more than 400 books and tracts, but he is best remembered for *Moll Flanders* and *Robinson Crusoe*.

8 See excerpts from Astell's "Serious Proposal to the Ladies" (1694), and "Reflections on Marriage" (1706), in Reynolds, *Learned Lady*, pp. 297-311. See also Thomas Woody, *History of Women's Education in the United States* (Lancaster, Pa: The Science Press, 1929) 2 vols., I, pp. 28-29, 156. Woody is a primary source for Chapter 7.

9 R. K. Root (ed.). *Lord Chesterfield's Letters to His Son* (New York: E. P. Dutton & Co., 1929) pp. 63-67.

10 Mary Wollstonecraft, *A Vindication of the Rights of Women* (London: J. Johnson, 1792; reprint ed., New York: Source Book Press, 1971) pp. 15-58, 99-131. See also, Eleanor Flexner, *Mary Wollstonecraft* (New York: Coward, McCann & Geoghegan, 1972) p. 155, 163. Fordyce told women in his sermons to be more tender and respectful toward their husbands, to study their humors, overlook their mistakes, and submit to their opinions. See his *Sermons to Young Women* (Philadelphia: Thomas Dobson, 1787) pp. 76-77, 161-62. Although the bugbear of homosexuality constantly followed Wollstonecraft (a woman wanting a man's education was naturally suspect), she very decidedly preferred the opposite sex. In giving birth to radical thinker William Godwin's "love child" (and dying in the process), she created a sensation in Europe and America. In later years the "love

127

child," Mary II also became a writer (*Frankenstein*), and her elopment with the married poet Percy Shelly was equally an international scandal.

[11] Luther Weeks Courtney, "Hannah More's Interest in Education and Government," *The Baylor* (Texas) *Bulletin* 32 (December, 1929); 10-16, 22-23. See also, Mary Alden Hopkins, *Hannah More and Her Circle* (New York: Longmans, Green and Co., 1947) pp. 172-80, 203-05, 265. In her thirties, More was a *femme savant*, a best-selling poet and playwright, and a toast of London society. Later, though, she "settled on spinsterhood," took the courtesy title "Mrs."— which *successful* middle-aged *single* women were permitted to do—and devoted the rest of her life to girls' and mass education. Many American Sunday Schools (reading and writing schools) were modeled after her school in the village of Cheddar, which came to be known for its cheeses.

[12] Erasmus Darwin, *A Plan for the Conduct of Female Education in Boarding Schools* (London: J. Drewry, 1797 and Philadelphia, 1798; reprint ed., New York: Johnson Reprint Corporation, 1968) pp. 1-12, 32-39, 66-68, 88. The Winthrop quote is in Earle, *Child Life*, p. 90.

[13] Sojourner Truth, the Negro Abolitionist and advocate for women's rights (1790-1883) poked fun at the idea that men had ever been chivalrous or gallant to the great majority of women. As a slave, she wrote, she had "ploughed, planted and worked as much as any man," and had " borne the lash" as well. She had "birthed 13 children" only to see most of them sold off into slavery—"with no one to hear me bawl," she said, "but Jesus."

[14] To keep order and good discipline, teachers sometimes made boys sit on the girls' side of the room. The mere threat of such a humiliation was usually enough the calm the roughest rowdy. See Woody, *History of Women's Education*, pp. 144-48.

[15] The admission of girls to the new high schools is in Edward A. Krug, *The Shaping of the American High School* (New York: Harper & Row, 1964) pp. 11-12, 171-72, 229-30, 279, 299.

[16] Edward H. Clarke, *Sex in Education* (Boston: James R. Osgood & Co., 1873; reprint ed. NY: Arno Press

and the *New York Times*, 1972) pp. 118-161. The entrance of females into medical, law and theological schools is in Woody, *History of Women's Education*, v. 2, pp. 340-381.

[17] "The School Mistress," *Harper's Magazine* (June-November, 1878, LVII (57) pp. 607-611.

[18] "Women in the Eighties," *Ladies Home Journal*, November, 1979, pp. 69-74.

EIGHT
For the Few—or the Many?

"Quo Vadis?"

Henryk Sienkiewicz
1895

As the 350th anniversary of American education approaches, a host of number-counters across the land may well puff with pride. More than 42,600,000 children are enrolled in public elementary and secondary schools. They attend classes in 86,500 school buildings in 16,000 autonomous school districts. They are taught by 2,200,000 teachers, two-thirds of whom are women. They are taught at the annual cost of $81 billion, about $2,000 per student per year, 5% of the Gross National Product. Seventy-six percent of these children are white, 16% are black, and 8% are of Hispanic or other origin. More than half of them are transported to and from school at public expense. School attendance is mandatory throughout the land, usually to age 16, although enforcement of attendance laws varies widely from school district to school district. On the average, students attend school 165 days per year—up from 99 days at the beginning of the century.

In 1950, less than 50% of United States students were being graduated from high school. Today, the figure exceeds 80% and is still climbing. In 1950, only 10% of black students were graduated from high school; that figure now exceeds 70%. In 1910, the average 24-year-old American had completed only eight years of schooling, in 1950, only nine years; but the figure now stands at 12.3 years, thanks in part to dropout prevention programs. The United States has more of its 15-18-year-olds enrolled in schools than any other country in the world. About three-fourths of them earn high school diplomas—up from about one-third in depression years, and from one-half during the 1950's. Twenty-five percent of those graduating from high school earn a college degree. In the process, moreover, students are exercised, fed, and given experience in manipulating the electronic equipment on which their future will depend.[1]

But these "bottom line" numbers do not alter the obvious fact that the *quality* of American education is still negotiable, still subject to inertia, erosion, and undisguised assault, or the fact that for all these "strengths," the American school is still vulnerable to those reactionaries who would "close it down," who would, had they the means, reverse the "opening up" process described in these pages. There seem to be as many opponents of the secularization of schools now, for example, as there were in the time of Franklin and Mann. The Constitution, the mandates of the Congress, and the judgments of the Supreme Court have not diminished the purpose of the so-called fundamentalists— indeed those laws have roused them to greater fury. Moral absolutists have redefined the centuries-old term "humanism" to mean the very opposite of its historical connotation of learning. Employing it as a "buzz-word," they see all things through a glass darkly: relativist philososphy, biological sciences, realism in human relations and in the expression thereof. Concentrating on the schools, they ignore the history highlighted in this volume and claim that educators have abandoned a neutral stance to become wholly "anti-God."

As before, the tenets of the absolutists are prayer and Bible reading. Their arguments repeat certainties about inspiration and discipline. As did the Puritans, they view children as damned if not saved, and salvation as paramount to learning. With modern ingenuity, however, they adopt the true humanist's call for fullness, not only culturally but in method as well. How can children see the *whole* of life if they are not shown religious truths? Modernist also in their use of the media, they cite polls declaring that three out of four Americans favor "voluntary" prayer and Bible readings in

132

the public schools. Although the Supreme Court of the United States forbade teaching religion in public schools by representatives of private groups, Massachusetts school children were, in 1980, praying aloud in their public schools by virtue of a ruling of a state supreme court that students were suffering "no irreparable harm." Keystone High School students at Lagrange, Ohio, listen daily over a public address system to their principal's recitation of the Lord's Prayer. "If anyone wants to sit there and read a book," he says, "they don't have to participate." Caddo Parish, Louisiana, children have never stopped praying. The implications of such practices are stunning; so are the "what-ifs" of the "inspirational" messages conveyed to students at sport rallies, commencements and holiday activities.

Still unsettled in courts or in public opinion are the field campaigns of Christian youth groups on school campuses. Young Life, a Colorado Springs based quasi-religious organization is but one example. Employing the techniques of media-gloss, thirtyish, often blue-jeaned proselytizers are coming into school buildings in almost every state, immersing themselves, where welcome, in the life of the school, attending pep rallies, table-hopping in the school cafeteria, hanging posters, organizing dances and skiing trips, recruiting, "rapping," and counseling with students, and suggesting Christian solutions to teen-age problems. In Dallas (Texas) County schools alone, eight Youth ministers work the public schools on a daily basis telling the children, as one minister recently put it, "that Christ loves them." At nearby Richardson (Texas) High School, Young Life ministers hold Bible meetings in classrooms after school hours, on the ground (as one administrator recently put it) that "if the school can sponsor dances, it can certainly sponsor prayer meetings." Owing to the organization's influence at Highland Park High in Dallas' most exclusive neighborhood, students recently voted to reinstate Bible reading at the school by a vote of 881-27. Prayer at pep rallies is a 40-year tradition, and one administrator has recently said that the rallies are optional and "if the prayers offend students, they don't have to go to the pep rally."

Probably nowhere in the world has the issue of the

proper relationship of religion and public education been more complex than in the United States. The situation continues to be characterized by confusion and anxiety about what may and may not be done in the public schools under the First Amendment. Still to be determined is whether the battle will continue to focus merely on prayers and Bible readings, or whether it will shift to the more important question of proselytizing on public school campuses.[2]

The absolutists' campaigns have also inspired a resurgence of "book burning" hardly a generation after Hitler and Herr Goebbels. Again using the Orwellian technique that made "humanism" mean "Godlessness," the would-be censors insist that concerned citizens have a "right to select" school textbooks and certain library books. Many schools have become a battleground in a struggle over social, family and political values, much of the fight centering on which books shall be used in the public schools. Even staid, placid, healthy, middle-class communities in New York, West Virginia, Indiana, Oklahoma, Texas, and Georgia have been caught up in destructive book battles in which teachers have been fired, student newspapers shut down, and thousands of schoolbooks burned in bonfires fed by smug moralizers. In these instances, truth is self-righteously trampled. "Most public school textbooks are nothing more than Soviet propaganda," the "Moral Majority's" Reverend Jerry Falwell has recently told a radio-television audience of more than a milion in the presence of five U.S. senators. "Our atheistic schools are destroying our children's moral values." No student of history, he urged parents to "rise up in arms and throw out every textbook that does not accurately present the American heritage." While the magnitude of this anti-schoolbook movement is easily underestimated, a nationwide survey sponsored by the American Library Association, the Association of American Publishers, and the Associaton of Supervision and Curriculum Development points to the involvement of more than 3,200 of the nation's school districts and more than 26,950 of its school libraries in challenges to literay works and textbooks. During 1981 alone, according to the ALA's Office for Intellectual Freedom, more than 100 titles were removed or threatened with removal from school and public libraries in more than 30 states.

There is a vague but widespread suspicion that school-books have strayed too far from traditional values, and that because of this children can no longer emerge from public schools morally unscathed. These views are supported across a broad spectrum of society, not just the political or religious Right. Many well-meaning, well-educated, well-organized and well-financed citizens groups are joining today's anti-book crusade in a resurgence of reactionist thought reminiscent of the World War I period. Among their numbers are thousands of ordinary citizens who see society moving—they know not quite how—in the wrong direction; who, unable to deal with the changes, feel impotent and alienated.

The first premise of the ultra-moralists is generally acceptable. Children really do need guidance in schools before they encounter the ubiquitous problems of drug use, promiscuity and crime . But they raise that shield from horizon to horizon: Children need to be protected and shielded from books that ridicule their faith or subvert their family relationships. They need positive heroes and role models not cynical works that defame historical figures by revealing their weaknesses. Childhood is a time of joy, and there should be very little in books, therefore, in the way of unhappy endings; certainly nothing they read should be pervasively sad. Nothing smacking of anti-government, anti-parent or anti-Christian sentiment has any place in the school. After all, parents pay the bills for education, and by rights they should also have a say in what happens at school. Certainly, books depicting unorthodox family arrangements, sexual explicitness, speculations about religion or unflattering portraits of authority or corporate or business practices have no place in the school, they say. In fact, no book belongs in the school which one would not welcome in his home; the school is not a peddler of smut—and works with sexual themes, however "educational," have no place.

The books most opposed today in American schools are those dealing with ecology, environment, consumerism, world geography (if there is mention of one-worldism), world history (if Marx and Lenin are not discredited), works that deal with conflicts between parents and children (parents cannot be portrayed as hypocritical or in any other negative way), and the so-called "dirty word" books, including the *American Heritage Dictionary*, the *Merriam-Webster New Collegiate Dictionary* (because of 70 or 80 "obscene" words), and the *Dictionary of American Slang*. Also opposed are books that do not champion the work ethic or promote patriotism or the family unit as the basis of American life; books about pagan cultures and lifestyles; and ethnic studies, particularly if they involve the use of non-standard English. Neither should books overemphasize Vietnam or Watergate; and works of homosexuals should be excluded altogether—including the works of Emily Dickinson, Gertrude Stien, John Milton, Willa Cather, Virginia Woolf, Hans Christian Andersen, Tennessee Williams, Walt Whitman, Marcel Proust, Oscar Wilde, Horatio Alger, Jr., T. E. Lawrence, Truman Capote, Jean Genet, Somerset Maugham, Gore Vidal and Rod McKuen.

Titles most often banned or complained about in today's schools include *The Scarlet Letter, A Farewell to Arms, The Sound and the Fury, The Grapes of Wrath, The Catcher in the Rye, Flowers for Algernon, Soul on Ice, For Whom the Bell Tolls, 1984, Brave New World, Huckleberry Finn, Catch 22,* and *Portnoy's Complaint.* One of the largest textbook and schoolbook "review" organizations in the United States objects to Sir Walter Scott's *Ivanhoe,* Alfred, Lord Tennyson's *The Foresters,* and Howard Pyle's *Merry Adventures of Robin Hood* on the ground that these works depict Robin Hood as a "folk hero," and not the traducer of property that he really was![3]

Pressure groups who otherwise object to the intrusion of even state government in the "local" matter of education, propose statutory tinkering with school curriculums to reflect their particular ideologies. Legislators will lose no support at the polls if, as has occurred in a dozen states, they add courses that emphasize "the essentials and benefits of the free enterprise system." But the absolutists now demand that the Biblical account of the creation be presented in biological sciences classes, not exclusively, they emphasize, but as a matter of giving "equal time," of "balancing" the theory of evolution. Unlike the situation at the time of the "monkey trial" in the 1920's, most legislators are now educated enough to know that there is no science in the arguments of the creationists and that religious concepts are philosophies, matters of faith, and not within the realm of logical method. But because of their readiness to extend their jurisdictions and their preoccupation with their own political security, many legislators are giving serious attention to the arguments of the"creationists."[4]

There are glaring inconsistencies in the absolutists' profession of seeking a "balance" in the teaching of biological sciences. The same groups who sponsor censorship on the grounds that young minds cannot discern right from wrong are in this case offering to let those same learners choose between two theories of evolution and creation! Just as they use the word "voluntary" in the call for school prayers, they seem to advocate a permissiveness in the process of learning that they denounce in all other social subjects. But by its very nature a school cannot be intellectually neutral. It is not merely a source of information; learning is based upon making judgments, and teaching is the catalyst in that process.

To shrug off the pressures of the absolutists as merely hypocritical is to grievously underestimate their basic quality. They are anti-human terrorists seeking to undermine not only the separation of church and state that is fundamental to American democracy, but to replace social harmonies with pious totalitarianism. Their own privately financed educational institutions are today's forums for the racism and classism of previous centuries. One only need review daily headlines to recognize the persistence of bigotries—segregation in housing, discrimination in the job market, anti-busing campaigns and amendments—that are quite apart from economic hardships or the inability of courts to process or guarantee enforcement of democratic laws. The momentum for equal treatment during preceding decades has slowed—or has been slowed—in part because of the implications for entrenched segments of the society of "opening up" public education to blacks and women.[5]

In Topeka, scene of *Brown v. Board*, black parents are back in court after nearly a third of a century claiming that schools are still segregated; that facilities at predominantly black schools are inferior to those at the mostly white schools, and that the best of Topeka's three high schools is still 96% white. In Little Rock, scene of a 1950's integration fight, public schools are 64% black, even though blacks make up only 34% of the city's population, signaling a phenomenon called "white flight." And the Dallas public schools are still among the most segregated in the nation with 66 of its 186 schools "'one race" schools in which more than 90% of the students are of a single race. Nationwide, nearly half the 11 million black, Hispanic and other minority children still attend public schools that are at least moderately segregated, and in the Northeast and North Central regions of the country, two out of every three minority students attend moderately segregated schools. In the once segregated Southeast, only a third of the minority students are now attending such schools.[6]

The unstable condition of one segment of American society surely marks a malaise that characterizes the spirit of the whole. Public confidence in all education has been eroded by the two irresistible developments of our time: ungoverned, complex economic burdens and the expansion, if not bursting forth, of population. Although some communities support programs for the variously disadvantaged, and generously extend school facilities to adults, many more repeatedly reject tax levies. Those seeking explanations for truancy and crime in the classrooms readily point to teachers' salaries and methods. The flourishing of private academies seems to threaten the purpose of education in a democracy just as that development did in the day of Horace Mann. The curricula of these schools are, however, far more ideological and hostile to democratic values than ever before. Instead of recognizing the danger of such domestic subversion, governmental leaders are ready to encourage their growth by extending favorable tax arrangements and by adopting "economy cuts" that stifle public education.[7]

Of all the ironies in the "opening up" story of the

American school, the final and indeed the saddest is this: that the very class of citizen Horace Mann's ideological heirs fought so desperately to elevate through schooling over the past 140 years, the class which historically has profited most from the school, and which stands to gain the most by its continuance, now stands most ready to "close down" the school. This class would deny the school's benefits not only to new constituencies, such as alien children, but (suicidally it seems) to itself as well. Wittingly and unwittingly, thousands of ordinary citizens, themselves products of the school (yet another irony), threaten to lay waste to all that has been gained on their behalf. Oblivious to the many perils to public education, they take it for granted. Unwary, they support competing "Christian" academies and tax-credit schemes. Unmindful that they erode the very process they wish to improve—education—they tamper with the school's curriculum, rendering it sterile. They would water down science with "creationism;" water down English and literature by censoring out Mark Twain and Gore Vidal; water down social studies with their watchful eyes on textbooks and cocked ears to the treatment of controversial issues. It is but a small part of this larger irony that so many religionists (who *established* the school in the 1630's and ran it for 200 years) are now withdrawing their children from public schools and re-enrolling them in vastly inferior "Christian" academies, owing (again an irony) to racial mix and a percieved anti-God stance on the part of the public school.

But American education faces "the best of times" as well as "the worst of times." Developments in telecommunications are revolutionizing access to information, potentially enabling any person to acquire a level of knowledge heretofore reserved for those who could attend Groton or Harvard.[8] It remains only for us to be sure than in that individualization of learning at the television screen, the purpose of education as the foundation of democracy is not further fragmented, and that the new technology does not ultimately dispense with the judgments offered by the teachers and the "mixture" provided by the classroom. Otherwise, the essential qualitative needs of American society—those needs that have been met by the efforts of educators for 350 years—will be sacrificed to meet the requirements of that tyrant, King Numbers.

Eight

[1] W. Vance Grant and Leo J. Biden, *Digest of Educational Statistics*, 1980 (Washington, D.C.: U.S. Government Printing Office, 1980) pp. 14, 34, 51-61.

[2] On the school and religion is in Debbie K. Solomon, "Highland Park Group Working to Revive Prayer in School," *Dallas Times Herald*, December 14, 1981; "Courts to Hear Latest Arguments on Voluntary School Prayer," *Phi Delta Kappan* 61, (April, 1980): 572; and "Religion and the Public Schools," *Curriculum Report of the National Association of Secondary School Principals* (NASSP) (Washington, D.C.: NASSP, June, 1979. See also *America* (April 28, 1979): 344.

[3] On schoolbook censorship is in James E. Davis, ed., *Dealing With Censorship* (Urbana, Illinois: National Council of Teachers of English Press, 1979) pp. 1-49, 220-21; Stephen Arons, "Book Burning in the Heartland," *Saturday Review*, July 21, 1979, pp. 24-29; Edward B. Jenkinson, "Protest Groups Exert Strong Impact," *Publishers Weekly*, February 12, 1979, p. 45; Stephen Arons, "The Crusade to Ban Books," *Saturday Review*, June 1981, pp. 16-19; "The Textbook Debate," *Newsweek*, December 17, 1979, pp. 102-03; "The Growing War: Pro and Anti-Censorship Forces Use Schools as Battlegrounds," *Phi Delta Kappan* 61 (June, 1980): 722; Colin Campbell, "Book Banning in America," *New York Times Book Review*, December 20, 1981; and Clifford A. Hardy, "Censorship and the Curriculum," *Educational Leadership* 31 (October, 1973): 10-11, 13. See also Arnie Weissmann, "Building the Tower of Babel," *Texas Outlook* 65 (Winter 1981-82): 10-15, 29-31.

[4] The issue of evolution and "creation science" is in Harvey Siegel, "Creationism, Evolution and Education: The California Fiasco," *Phi Delta Kappan* 62 (October 1981): 95-97; Thomas J. Flygare, "The Case of Segraves v. State of California," *Phi Delta Kappan* 62 (October1981): 98-101; "Creationism, Evolution and the Schools," *Church and State* 34 (May 1981): 108-110; "Scientists Ridicule 'Evidence' of Creationists," *Dallas Times Herald*, December 9, 1981; and

"Creation Law in Arkansas Struck Down," *Dallas Times Herald*, January 6, 1982. See also Claud P. Duet and John W. Newfield, "Legislative Influence on School Curriculum," *Peabody Journal of Education* 56 (October 1978): 38-40, and J. Charles Park, "Preachers, Politics, and Public Education: A Review of Right-Wing Pressures Against Public Schooling in America," *Phi Delta Kappan* 61 (May 1980): 608-15.

[5] These relevent current issues are discussed in David L. Moberly, "Compulsory Attendance: A Second Look," *The High School Journal* 63 (February, 1980): 195-99; "Small Schoolhouses That Won't Fade Away," *U.S. News & World Report*, September 10, 1979, p. 38; Ralph J. Kane, "The Mindless Box: The Case Against the American Classroom," *Phi Delta Kappan* 60 (March, 1979): 502-03: Elaine Yaffe, "Public Education: Society's Band-Aid," *Phi Delta Kappan* 61 (March, 1980): 452-4; Michael W. Kirst, "The Rationale for Public Schools," *Phi Delta Kappan* 63 (November, 1981): 164-5; Karen Hill-Scott and J. Eugene Grigsby, "Some Policy Recommendations for Compensatory Education," *Phi Delta Kappan* 60 (February, 1979): 443-5; "Help! Teachers Can't Teach," *Time*, June 18, 1980, pp. 89-92; Arthur W. Combs, "Humanistic Education: Too Tender For A Tough World?" *Phi Delta Kappan* 62 (February, 1981): 446-7; Gary Hoban, "The Untold Golden State Story: Aftermath of Proposition 13," *Phi Delta Kappan* 61 (September, 1979): 18-21; James L. Jarrett, "Toward Elitist Schools," *Phi Delta Kappan* 60 (May, 1979): 647-9; and Isaac Asimov, "A Cult of Ignorance," *Newsweek*, January 21, 1980, p. 19. See also "Tax-exempt Schools," *Dallas Times Herald*, January 12, 1982.

[6] Background for the section on desegregation reform and minority education in general is in "The Brown Decision: A Dream Deferred or a Dream Fulfilled?" *Ebony*, May 17, 1979 (25th year commemorative issue); "School Integration—A Long Way to Go," *U.S. News & World Report*, February 26, 1979, p. 13; "Making Magnets Draw," *Newsweek*, January 7, 1980, p. 68; "Linda Brown's Fight Goes On," *Newsweek*, December 10, 1979, p. 68; "Black Parents Claim Topeka Schools Still Segregated; Reopen *Brown* Case," *Phi Delta Kappan* 61 (November, 1979): 155; Bill Porterfield, "The Grief of Two Hometown Federal Judges," *Dallas Times Herald*, January 6, 1982; "Judge

Blasts Dallas' Efforts on Integration," *Dallas Times Herald*, January 5, 1982; and "Modest Changes for Little Rock Schools," *Arkansas Gazette*, December 24, 1981. See also "Texas vs. Alien Children," *Dallas Times Herald*, December 1, 1981; Thomas J. Flygare, "Illegal Alien Children Must Be Provided Free Public Education," *Phi Delta Kappan* 62 (February, 1981): 454; and Richard Burnett, "Illegal Aliens Come Cheap," *Progressive* 43 (October, 1979): 44-6.

[7] Some provocative essays on the condition of American education are: "Do Schools Stink? Why Not Quote the Sweet Facts?" *American School Board Journal* 167 (June, 1980): 20-21; Harold G. Shane, "An Educational Forecast for the 1980's," *Today's Education* 68 (April-May, 1979): 62-3; Harold Hodgkinson, "What's Right With Education," *Phi Delta Kappan* 61 (November, 1979).

[8] See "Education and the Telefuture," *Change* 11 (November-December 1979): 12-13.

INDEX

Makin, Bathusa Pell, 110
Mann, Horace, 46 ff, 73, 85
Margold, Nathan, 88
Marm schools, 4
Marshall, Thurgood, 90, 99
McLaurin, George, 93
"Mixed" schools, 74
More, Hannah, 114
Morgan, J. Pierpont, 72
Morgan, Junius, 71
Murray, Donald, 91
Myers, Gustavus, 72

National Association for Advancement,
  Colored People, 87
National Teachers' Assn
  (NEA), 68
New England Primer, 8

Opposition to public schools, 59-61

Peabody, George, 71, 73
People's Press, 70
Philadelphia Negro, 95
Phillips Academy, 31
Plessy v. Ferguson, 87
Public School Prayer, 133

Randolph, John, 67
Rate Bills, 66
Riggs, Elisha, 71
Roberts, Sarah, 85
Roberts v. City of Boston, 87
Rousseau, Jean Jacques, 108
Royal High School, 52

Santayana, George, 96
Schoolmaster, Colonial, 14
Sears, Barnas, 73
Segregation, 138
Sipuel, Ada, 93
Slater, John F., 72
Southern Education Foundation, 72